JEW BOY

Early praise for

JEW BOY

This is exceptionally well-written, brutal and honest, and not at all self-pitying. As someone who has known you for a very long time, I realize you hid your demons far better than I believed. You are absolutely right about your recurring theme ... none of us are alone.

—A U.S. Navy Master Chief Petty Officer

The writing is raw ... very raw. I empathized with your pains and fears and tastes for dear sweet smoothness to escape the shitholes and shitheads. I marvel at how either of us survived and didn't shoot anyone in the face.

—A U.S. Navy Master Chief Petty Officer

I know I'm being selfish, but I wanted more. You grabbed my attention and brought me along for the ride. You presented a phenomenal, gut-wrenching, honest look into the success you've become. I am convinced your story needs to be shared. I am convinced it will help others.

—RW, retired police officer & detective

JEW BOY

How I overcame beatings, porn, drugs, alcohol, suicide & high school to retire from the United States Navy

A MEMOIR OF SURVIVAL BY
'BABY MOUNTAIN FLOWER BEAR'

FORCE POSEIDON

LIMA DETROIT

ARTISANAL PUBLISHERS

FORTES · FORTUNA · ADIUVAT

FORCE POSEIDON

Force Poseidon is an imprint of Artisanal Publishers LLC
2981 Zurmehly Road, Lima Ohio 45806-1428
forceposeidon.com

This book is a work of narrative nonfiction.

Copyright ©2019 by Force Poseidon
on behalf of and for the benefit of 'Baby Mountain Flower Bear'

Cover copyright ©2019 by Force Poseidon
Library of Congress Cataloging-in-Publication Data has been applied for.

First Force Poseidon eBook edition
   March 2019 ISBN 978-0-578-47768-8
First Force Poseidon trade paperback
   March 2019 ISBN 978-0-578-47766-4

All rights reserved, including the right to reproduce this work or any
portion thereof in any form whatsoever, now or in the future, without
regard for form or method. For more information on the use of material
from this work (not including short excerpts for review purposes), please
see ForcePoseidon.com or address inquiries to Rights via email to
info@ForcePoseidon.com

Artisanal Publishers and Force Poseidon, by names and colophons, are
trademarks of Artisanal Publishers LLC. This book was produced in
Adobe InDesign CC 2019 using Adobe Garamond Pro for body copy
and jo_wrote_a_longsong designed by Lars Manenschijn for headings.

Piracy is theft. For information about special discount bulk purchases of
paper or ebooks, please contact Direct Sales via email to
info@ForcePoseidon.com, or write to Force Poseidon, 2981 Zurmehly
Road, Lima Ohio 45806-1428

Manufactured in the United States of America.

This book is dedicated to those who could not escape their demons. I hope my story helps others find the strength to make their escape.

PROLOGUE

HI. I'M WHITE NIGGER JEW BOY ALICE.

Psychologists and therapists over the years have suggested I write this story. I always resisted before, but now I feel like it's time to let all of this go and finally get on with the happy life that seems to have happened when I wasn't looking.

Aside from memory, much of the early information was explained by my mother and her brother over the years, but that was then. We really don't talk much anymore.

This is my story of survival and success despite the odds against me—and the odds were steep. It's my hope that by sharing my story, I may save someone like me, or like you.

I'm not using any real names in this story, including my own. All of the people in this book are still alive, with the exception of my grandparents and possibly my biological father.

People who know me or my extended family may be able to connect the dots and figure out who I'm writing about, but if that's true, those people already know much of this story and my writing it down changes nothing for them.

The story is about my own coming to terms with success while still believing I don't deserve what I've achieved. Among other topics, this book comes to terms with my struggles correlating pornography, sexual relationships, and genuine love.

This book is also about coming to terms with my past in a way that, unhappily, I think many people can relate to.

A modest warning: My life never pulled any punches on me, and I don't pull any punches writing about it. Some of these memories are still raw and afflicting. I write about them in the same language and with the same passion as the events themselves. If my life offends you, stop reading about it.

This story is for everyone like me.

This story is for everyone like you.

You are not alone.

"Baby Mountain Flower Bear"
January 2019

CHAPTER ONE
THE BASICS

I never met my father. I have no blood relation to my last name. My mom's first husband was her piano teacher, and nearly twice her age. I'm certain he took advantage of her, or at least the situation. My mom was fourteen and he was in his mid-twenties.

He often passed her around like a party favor and enjoyed watching his friends fuck her, using her like a sex doll. This is how I entered the world. I think I'm probably the son of the best man at their wedding.

My mom had it made growing up in ways I and my sister and brothers did not. Her parents were moderately financially successful when she grew up with her brother and sister in the woods of an East Coast state in the 1960s. She fell in love with her first husband right around the escalation of the Vietnam War.

She married him, the piano teacher, shortly after high school, at seventeen. No one in my mother's family liked him. He was fashionably anti-establishment and despised my grandparents for driving cars and living for "The Man."

He and my mother decided to join a commune just outside the Canadian border. This is where I was born in 1972. I was conceived by "Mountain Bear" and "Flower Bear." Those were seriously the hippie names they chose. So, there's the solved mystery of my unusual pen name.

I don't remember living in the commune. I was an infant. I know my mother was afraid of all the LSD and other drugs possibly entering my system, and her husband was treating her like crap—at one point in time he even fucked her sister. So, my mom and I left. What she tried to protect me from became my favorite chemical when I reached the age of fourteen. I loved acid. More on this later.

My mom left me with her parents after she left the commune. She started college, and slowly started working toward a nursing degree. My grandparents were awesome. I think I lived with them from the time I was less than a year old until I was about three. I'm almost fifty now, and I still have vivid memories of living there.

My grandmother had nine brothers and sisters. The house she grew up in was next door to the one-room schoolhouse she attended from kindergarten to twelfth grade, back around 1920. My grandmother grew up in the back woods and knew everything about that. She showed me how to pick wild mint, make walnut ice cream from scratch, make bread, make pretty much anything. She was energetic, funny, creative, and religious. She and my grandfather both were. She sang songs about Jesus a lot. They were really great people.

My grandfather was self-employed. He came from money, not a lot, but enough. He went to a good school and created a career as an independent contract estimator with his education. He and my grandmother settled on a decent property and had a pool, right on a lake. He was kind of a quiet, shy guy. I know he was a Mason, but not much else.

My fondest memories of him are how he held me when I would cry, because I never got that kind of affection at home. He would rock me and hum. I still remember the stubble on his cheeks as he held me, and the smell of cigarette smoke on his flannel shirt. It was pretty cool staying with them as I aged, too. I stayed there a lot.

My mom returned when I was three and I gained a "dad." I didn't know I was missing a dad. I just thought this guy was my dad. Well, my mom and "dad" took me away from my grandmother's house to a farm. The house was a duplex. We weren't poor back then, but it was certainly different than what I was used to. I don't remember much about that house. I think I blocked a lot of it out. I know the man hit me. He bragged about it later on in my life. I know he "hit me so hard, I went flying across the room" after I had apparently hit my mother in the stomach with a plastic cow when she was pregnant with my sister. He would retell this story frequently over the years.

After my sister was born, I filled her crib full of stuffed animals. I might have been trying to suffocate her, I don't know. I was maybe four. I vividly remember doing this, though, and I got in trouble for it.

I didn't enjoy living on the farm. I have a few memories that stick out: I remember seeing my dad leaving on a drill weekend with the National Guard. I also remember my mom running over one of our cats while backing out of the driveway. I remember seeing it thrash back and forth in the dirt. Gives me an eerie feeling thinking about it now.

We didn't live on the farm for very long. Two years later, we moved into a big, Victorian-style house in a really nice town. My middle brother was born shortly after we moved in. My dad's dad owned a farm-equipment sales and repair shop just outside of our backyard, and my dad worked there as a manager and mechanic.

Unfortunately, I remember everything about living in that house. I was probably six or so when I came home from school and saw what I now know was a bankbook on the dining room table. The statement had my first and middle names (real names) and a last name I didn't recognize. I asked my mom about the names and she immediately called her husband at work. I don't know what their conversation was about in great detail, but I understand now that she was informing him that she was going to tell me he wasn't my real dad.

I will never forget how that phone conversation ended. My mom slammed down the phone and yelled, "That asshole is not your father!" It turned out the last name I was using was my dad's, but my legal name was my mother's first husband's. I was registered for school under "my dad's" name. When I turned eighteen and registered for the draft, I had to use my legal name. So, I have an alias. My life was forever changed that confusing day. There would be other such days down the road.

Before I knew the truth, I used to wish he wasn't my real dad. Finding out he wasn't was kind of a relief. Him knowing that I found out was a fucking nightmare.

To say my dad started treating me different after that is an understatement. He outright resented me. He hated me. I was kept separated from my sister and brother. They could play together, and I could watch. He would coddle them, and tell me go do things for him, like get him a beer. I got him lots of beer. He would drink a case of beer in a night.

Life in that house was fucking bizarre. Just the house itself was fucking bizarre. My grandmother called our upstairs bathroom "Grand Central Station" for the traffic around it. And it was. It was the central part of the upstairs and all but one of the bedrooms led right into it.

And my parents never wore clothes at home.

I'd get out of the shower and my mom would be shitting on the toilet while my naked dad would be shaving before work, coughing up phlegm from the two packs of cigarettes he smoked every day and complaining about how hungover he was.

The nudity in the house didn't really bother me as a young kid. In fact, none of this bothered me until I was old enough to stay over friend's houses. I got to see how their parents behaved. I was able to start developing my own sense of what was fucked up and what wasn't. By about age ten or so, I had come to the conclusion that routine parental nudity in front of children was fucked up.

As my sister and brother got older, we had a pretty tight bond. We did a lot of stuff together, but it wasn't all fun. Part of our bond was our bondage: giving back, scalp, foot, and shoulder rubs to our dad while he was naked on his bed at night and my mom worked her evening shift as a nurse. The more I think about these scenes, the more disturbing they become.

When I say older, I think I was about eight, my sister was five and my brother was four. It never occurred to me to tell my mom about what was going on. I didn't know what was right or wrong at this point. I'm not entirely sure my mom knew. I do remember her asking me to rub her feet once in a while. She wasn't naked when I was rubbing her feet. I seem to remember she was wearing socks. I think.

My dad (I know I'm not calling him step-dad; he was the only dad I knew then) started running the house like an Army barracks and right around this time, age eight or so, I started getting the nicknames. My first nickname was Alice.

Alice was awkward at sports. Alice didn't like doing shots of whiskey, and once got punched for declining an offer. Alice would cry when dad would come into the living room while I watched TV and pull my hair until I cried and then call me Alice. Dad didn't like Alice and Alice didn't know why.

Alice didn't like dad, either.

One day, Alice found his dad's porn stash. It wasn't hard to find—it was practically everywhere my dad kept his stuff. He was gone on an overnight trip the first time when I saw the tip of the iceberg that was his porn collection. I was sleeping on the floor of my parents' bedroom inches away from a stack of magazines that caught my attention. The first magazine I opened displayed an image of two women in a sixty-nine position at the breast level, each sucking each other's breasts. I didn't feel sexually excited over that image, but the shock value of it has stayed with me for about forty years.

Finding that magazine led to looking elsewhere for porn, like a weird scavenger hunt. Under his bed were stacks of porn—magazines, books, playing cards, even reel-to-reel movies. The playing cards are ingrained in my mind because they were old-school. All of the women were super hairy.

His Army foot locker at the end of his bed was packed with porn. His nightstand was packed with porn. His closet ... porn. I saw so much porn as a kid that I've had what I can only describe informally as sexual Attention Deficit Disorder ever since. To be clear, I haven't been clinically diagnosed as such, but I'm giving a copy of this book to my current psychologist, who can maybe help sort all of this out. I've never before told all of what's in this book in such detail to anyone.

The bottom line here is that I cannot just focus on who I'm with. I wrestle with images I've seen every time I have sex. It's frustrating. I never even masturbated to the porn I found. I didn't start masturbating until much later, perhaps not even until after I turned twenty.

One thing stayed constant: "Alice," "Jew Boy," and eventually "White Nigger"—all my dad's personas for me over the years—were *angry*. I fucking *hated* that man I called "dad." I prayed he would die almost every night. I thought about killing him all the time—every fucking day. I most often considered shooting him while he slept.

One night, he woke me from a sound sleep. He asked if I remembered standing in his bedroom. I did not. He said I walked into his bedroom, stood next to his bed and repeated, over and over, *"I did half. I did half. I did half."* I don't know what it meant, but to this day, I think that was a warning that I could have killed him.

I'm almost certain this sleepwalking episode was my one and only such occurrence. However, I did fake a sleepwalking episode much later. I'll get to that story in another chapter.

Dad always drank beer as we grew up, but he wasn't always violent early on. By the time I became "Jew Boy," he was violent. Jew Boy was a punching bag for emotional, mental, and physical abuse. And I still was forced to rub that naked man at night.

He was making very little money, and the money he made he spent on beer. My mom was bringing home the bulk of the money to put the food on the table while my dad spent his days drinking beer.

He was resentful about this, and at times his violence erupted because of it.

CHAPTER TWO
ALICE

Even as "Alice," I could have been a good kid, but I wasn't always a good kid. Alice once smashed all of the windows out of his parent's garage with a baseball bat. The windows were antique and irreplaceable. Alice didn't do that out of anger. He thought it was funny. Alice went back to his grandmother's house for a while after that.

I was four.

When I came back, things were weirder. "Alice" always had a hollow pit in his stomach when he came back home, like something was really, really wrong. And something was. My dad didn't like Alice. Alice just didn't quite realize yet how much.

I grew up around a lot of guns. Me and "dad" shot a lot of guns. This meant there were a lot of guns to clean and maintain, and that man taught "Alice" to clean them so he wouldn't have to. Alice was very good at cleaning guns and shooting guns. Alice was about six or seven when he started cleaning guns, which pleased his "dad," but he was still Alice.

When my mom married my "dad," she went with the polar opposite of her hippie-child first husband. That guy was a hippie through and through.

My "dad," her second husband, was an Army-trained, Vietnam-era grunt, and he was very proud of that status. He didn't go to Vietnam, though, which I think was something that always bothered him. I think it made him question his *machismo.*

I know it bothered him that he didn't make the Army a career. He would get drunk and depressed and repeatedly say, "If I had just stayed in, I'd be retired by now." Those words stuck with me for the rest of my life. I didn't want that kind of regret.

I didn't want to become him.

So, I liked guns. "Alice's" first gun was a Daisy Model 880 Powerline 10-pump BB gun. Alice could put a BB through a penny from twenty-five feet away. Alice was learning land navigation on weekends. Alice was being raised as a soldier. Alice had a terrible sense of direction and had a hard time understanding how to read a compass.

I wasn't really being trained, just told to use a compass to figure out how to get home from a day out shooting guns and driving around in the woods in my dad's 1970 Jeep Scout.

Training in the woods was really just an excuse for my dad to get drunk again. He would bring a case of beer, guns, and my brother and me for weekend adventure—every weekend. Out there, he would ignore his other son while giving "Alice" a hard time.

He didn't want his other son to be a soldier. He wanted me to be a soldier because he wanted "Alice" out of his life by eighteen. I wasn't able to see it then, but it's clear now. He had plans for me.

And those plans were to fight the Russians.

During the Cold War, my dad stockpiled weapons in the house against an invasion of Russian paratroopers. Weapons were literally hidden all over the house. If you opened the cupboard to grab a towel after a shower, you would see rifles along the back of the shelving. Take your pick. There were boxes of ammo in there, too.

My second gun was a single-shot twelve-gauge, and I can't remember the manufacturer. It was a gift from my dad for my tenth birthday. It was light but kicked like a mule. I cried the first time I shot it and my dad ridiculed me to no end. I was the quintessential "Alice" to him at that moment.

I spent most of the rest of our weekends cleaning his guns, doing chores, getting him a beer from the fridge every fifteen minutes, and getting laughed at and shoved around because that gun had kicked the shit out of me. I remember this episode caused me a great deal of embarrassment and anger. I was trying *so hard* to gain acceptance from this man. I craved having a real dad who would love me and do things with me because he wanted to, not as an excuse for drunkenness and abuse. And I was stuck with this fucking bully.

Then *he* fired the gun. His reaction surprised me. That gun hurt him, too, and he was a big man. He stood there rubbing his shoulder and grinning in shock.

"Goddamn, that hurt!" Asshole.

He didn't fire it from his shoulder ever again. He would show off that he could handle the kick by shooting it from his hip. I wasn't allowed to shoot it that way.

When we got home later that day, I went to get in the shower. My mom was in the bathroom taking a shit. When I took my shirt off she freaked out. My bicep to my shoulder was bruised green and purple from shooting that damned gun.

My dad walked out his bedroom, saw my arm, and said something about how "Alice" was crying like a girl over it. I think my mom was scared of him. I could tell she was mad, but she didn't say anything. She rarely did.

And I think she was scared for me, too. My dad was getting more violent around then. I think he really started to turn up the resentment that I wasn't his kid, and that I knew it. I didn't look anything like him and he couldn't hide it anymore. But that didn't stop his drive for me to join the military. I think it only increased that drive.

"The military is going to make a *man* out of you, Alice."

And my gun collection grew. I had four firearms right near my bed and in the drawer of my homework desk—just in case I had to fight the Russians. The 1984 movie *Red Dawn* was like his fucking Book of Revelations.

At fourteen, I got my hunting license. That twelve-gauge was the shotgun I had to hunt with, but I never was going shoot anything with it. There's just no way to get a hip shot from a tree stand. Animals were safe from me with that gun.

During breaks from school starting around age eleven, I started living in another state with my uncle every summer. My uncle was hilarious and I loved going there. My uncle was also a drunk, but he was the quintessential drunk funny uncle. He was not a good influence for me but I sure loved living with him then.

I wasn't "Alice" when I was with my uncle. In a lot of ways, he was like my dad. He had also served a few years in the Army as an artillery officer. He didn't serve in Vietnam either, and I don't think he regretted that one bit.

He still is an avid outdoorsman. We went fishing together every day when he got home from work. We camped almost every weekend. Shot guns fairly often. He had a decent collection like my dad, but my uncle collected a lot of antique firearms. Also like my dad, he used the woods as an excuse to get shitty drunk, too.

And just like my dad, he was racist as shit. Every racist joke I ever knew I learned from him. No one in my family ever liked anybody except white people. At age eleven I thought his jokes were funny. It bothers me that people my age today still laugh at jokes like that. They really aren't funny.

That's how I spent my summers from the time I was eleven until I was sixteen.

My absence each year did not make my dad's heart grow any fonder of my presence. Quite the opposite. It was a disappointment to him for me to return home. I can't escape that feeling of having a hollow pit of despair in my stomach returning to that environment. It still haunts me.

After my first summer trip to my uncle's, I had this crazy image in my head of returning home to a big *Welcome home!* banner and getting showered with affection and being told I was missed.

My mom was working that evening. I came home to no banners. I came home to no affection whatsoever. I entered the house to a fat, naked and drunk asshole who told me to go clean the dishes.

I felt so fucking dejected. So empty.

It never occurred me that time with my uncle was nothing more than my parents just getting rid of me for a few months. I never really thought about this until just now. I'm not even sure how I feel about it. There is a sense of resentment, but also a feeling that I no longer care, or at least I shouldn't. I think disappointment is the better word.

I'm disappointed with that man, my mother, and that whole family. I wouldn't be who I am today without them—and I am truly happy with who I've become—but I also can't help but think how much better a person I might have been with a family that made me feel loved as a kid.

It was around this time the chores increased in frequency and intensity. Cleaning the yard every once in a while was now an "asshole and elbows" event every Saturday morning. I washed his car every Saturday afternoon. I did all of the dishes. I got him all of his fucking beer. I was his personal TV remote control.

I would be outside in the yard playing with my brother and our neighbor's kid, who was my age, and my dad would yell from his bedroom for me to come inside, go upstairs and change the fucking channel on his TV.

His behavior became more intense; he was so fucking angry all the time. And his drinking was out of control. He was downing well over a case a day by this point. Bud Light. By the case. The only good news was that I lost the name Alice by my second return trip.

Enter "Jew Boy."

CHAPTER THREE
JEW BOY

I was twelve. My dad didn't have many friends. He had only one, actually. One day I met his friend's dad, who misunderstood my name. My dad laughed about it, and I was "Jew Boy."

I'm not Jewish. Well, probably I'm not. I think my biological father may have been Jewish. The name just seemed to fit, I guess.

Jew Boy was good enough to be written on full display of every lunch bag I carried to the school bus stop about a mile or so from my house. I used to pitch the bag in the same neighbor's yard every morning. He caught me once and didn't say anything.

All that was ever in the lunch bag was two pieces of bread—every morning. I wish the neighbor had said something.

I was just about to enter high school around the time our family money got tight. It was also right about this time when life got crazier for me. The farming business in the state was vanishing. Along with the disappearing farms came the sale of my dad's father's ag machines business.

I became a household slave. "Jew Boy" had chores. Jew Boy wasn't allowed to have friends. Jew Boy served the house.

I didn't want to have friends, at least at the house. Jew Boy was fucking embarrassed at how fucked up his home life was. Jew Boy was embarrassed about a lot of shit.

For instance, when his dad would mow the lawn on his riding mower with his cut-off jean shorts, no shirt and a fucking Hanes underwear waistband as a headband. I think he embarrassed the whole neighborhood. Sucking down beer after beer. Showing off his three patches of back hair—an enormous one on each shoulder blade and little island right below his neck. It makes me sick to think about all of this again.

I felt sick a lot as Jew Boy. I can't begin to describe the tightness in my abs to compensate for the fucking hollow feeling behind them.

I fucking hated to hear the words "shine like a nigger's heal," which my dad used to describe how he wanted things cleaned.

"Make those dishes shine like a nigger's heal."

"Wash my car and make it shine like ..."

"Clean these guns and ..."

Fuck I hated that dude. I had a fucking rage within me that only subsided when I eventually discovered the world of pot and acid.

Anyway, I was treated like shit. If Alice had it bad, Jew Boy had it fucking worse. And what about those fucking lunch bags, man. I felt so defeated. I felt fucking worthless. And then it got worse.

Dad had a "heart to heart" with Jew Boy one afternoon.

I was called from my room to have a seat on the living room steps across from my dad, who was sitting in a red chair with the arm charred black from being too close to the wood stove. Dad needed to have a serious conversation with Jew Boy. The talk is painful for me to bring up, but here it goes.

He said he and his father thought I was mentally underdeveloped, that something was mentally wrong with me. I loved my granddad. It crushed me to hear he thought I was stupid. Dad said he was thinking about putting me in a special school and I started crying because it was all so fucking overwhelming.

He stopped talking at that point and told me to go upstairs. He was successfully starting to break me. His cruelty was intentional and specific, and it fucking worked, man. It fucking worked.

It didn't help that by this time during school I had a black friend and a Mexican friend. My black friend was not allowed inside our house. My black friend stopped being my friend because of it. My Mexican friend was barely tolerated. I spent a lot of nights at my Mexican friend's house. He was a great friend then, and he is a really good man now.

In fact, I'll take a break from my story here to talk about him and his mom and his sister. His mom left his dad, who remained in Mexico City. She brought her son and daughter to a place that was almost 100 percent white redneck and they did not have an easy time. His sister had to finally return to Mexico. She hated living in this new environment. But my friend was awesome. He was always so positive and energetic. Everyone but my dad liked him. He helped me out in more ways than I can ever thank him for. He's a school teacher now, and I'll bet he's the best damned school teacher on the planet. Writing this just prompted me to post a note to his FB wall.

So, I was Jew Boy for all of eighth grade—and most of high school. Jew Boy had a violent streak and got in a few fights. Jew Boy did a lot of stupid shit. Jew Boy started acting out. My Mexican friend and I parted ways when I started hanging out with a new crowd because he wasn't looking for a means to escape his situation like I was. My new crowd liked drugs.

So did I.

I started high school and within the first month I found out about pot. I loved pot and it made me mellow out, but I still carried that fucking lunch bag with *Jew Boy* scribbled on it. Jew Boy wanted to kill the man who stood and watched me pack those bags with two pieces of bread wrapped in tinfoil. That's all the lunch I needed to pack. I figured I was just going to throw each bag over my neighbor's fence anyway, so why waste any more food?

The first time I smoked pot was in my freshman gym class. It was about three weeks into the school year. Our gym teacher was old and literally senile. I'm not joking. He was a former WWII U.S. Navy Sailor and had been a Golden Glove boxer, but he'd seen better days. And they'd been a long time ago.

This dude in my gym class walked up to me in the locker room one day and asked if I wanted to smoke a bowl. Sure. There was construction going on for a new track or parking lot or something, and there were giant dirt piles back there. We sprinted from the gym to behind a dirt pile, smoked a bowl, and learned each other's names. Then we joined the gym class that by now was outside playing touch football. We just showed up on the field and that gym teacher asked what team we were on. I said I didn't know.

"We've been out here for twenty minutes and you don't know what team you're on?" Nope. He didn't know why we didn't, of course.

I don't remember anything after that—or for the rest of that day. But I knew I liked to smoke a bowl. I definitely wanted more of that. I quickly found the right crowd to smoke with, which was pretty much all the time.

You could smoke cigarettes in high school back then, so I started smoking cigarettes, too. That made it easier to find pot. The high school smoking section was an open-air drug market, and you find pretty much anything you wanted. So, when I later wanted to try acid, I did. It made me feel like anything but Jew Boy.

When I discovered LSD, everything changed. I fucking loved acid. I took it as often as I could. I went to school high on acid. I would spend time with my family on acid. I acted normal on acid. Inside my head was a constant battle for sanity, but that was part of the fun. It was like a game of self-entertainment. I could physically exist, hold a conversation and the entire time be experiencing something completely unexplainable. I was leaving my drab world without really going anywhere. I was numb in every sense.

LSD was my vacation from being Jew Boy.

Acid made me feel warm inside. It actually reminded me of being held by mom's father, my real grandfather. I felt insulated from my pain and frustration. At times, I felt like I was on a relatively smooth train ride—just mild vibrations and a feeling of being in motion. I really enjoyed these feelings. The hallucinations weren't important, and at times became cumbersome. I didn't take acid for the hallucinations once I discovered that warmth. Although, as with any "acid head," I did enjoy seeing auras and trails. I didn't enjoy distortions or seeing objects that didn't look like they were supposed to.

I was all about the vibes. And I don't mean to glorify this drug.

It certainly isn't for just anyone. I have seen people on bad trips, and man, it isn't a cool scene to see someone shaking and sweating and shitting their pants—especially when it's just the two of you and you just wanted to have a good time, and now this is your life for the next eight or so hours. I never hung out with that pants-shitting dude again. I think he wanted to avoid me after that, anyway.

I took acid for the first time one morning before school, about a week or two after my first time smoking pot. I can't believe no one knew I was losing my mind on the inside. It was like I didn't really exist. I was present, but not there, you know? Everything was hilarious.

Then at lunchtime, the person who sold me the dose told other kids I'd taken it. Soon the cafeteria started chanting my name and it didn't bother me. I didn't freak out. I just sat there staring at everyone. The teachers in the cafeteria asked me what was going on, and I said I didn't know, and that was the extent of it. No one messed with me after that. They knew I was fucked up, and I think I impressed the shit out of them by not losing it.

I got a few jobs shortly thereafter, filling the hours between school I didn't care about and the home life I wanted to escape. I washed dishes. I delivered newspapers. I only worked to buy drugs. Drugs were my answer to Jew Boy.

I was fourteen and still spent my summers with my uncle, but I couldn't smoke cigarettes or pot or drop acid when I was with him so it just wasn't as fun. I still went hiking and fishing and camping, but it was getting boring. And my uncle wasn't as funny. Age and drugs made him different to me.

We stumbled across a marijuana grow site during a fishing trip. I didn't even know it was marijuana. He did. When he told me, my reaction and statement of, "You know how much money I could get at school with that?" did not go over well at all. In fact, I don't remember ever seeing him look disappointed in me before that.

By my sophomore year, I was ready to try all kinds of stuff. And I did. I tried all kinds of stuff. I can't list everything I tried because I can't remember it all, and I don't think I want to. That school year was a blur of drugs and shitty performance in school.

I do remember we got a dog during this timeframe. It was a

German Shepherd. I forget her name. My parents kept her tied up in the sand pile in the backyard. That dog was miserable just like every other being my parents were responsible for. She wanted to be free but was tethered to a metal pole. The symbolism here crushes me. I remember being happy when that dog was no longer in our yard.

My youngest brother was born around this time, but I don't really remember much about his childhood. I had to attend summer school that year and I missed the annual trip to my uncle's house. Instead, I saw the Grateful Dead at a local venue, and took a bus trip to see them again a few states away. My parents were not happy about any of that. I think they were getting hints of my growing rebellion and independence. My dad suspected I was on drugs, but never caught me with any. He said if he did, was going to shoot me. And I believed him.

He came close to catching me on several occasions, so that was exciting.

The first time was in our back yard. I was playing hacky sack with my brother and someone else. I don't remember who. My dad ran up from behind me, yelled "Drug bust!" and started putting his hands all over me like he was a cop frisking me. I freaked out. I didn't freak out often, but I had a half-ounce of pot in my underwear. I started acting like I was in pain to get him off me. He probably wouldn't have stopped if there wasn't an audience.

He searched my closet one morning and missed seeing the ounce of pot just inside my closet door. One time, he even prank-called me on my sister's phone and asked, "Hey man, you want to buy some drugs?" He sucked at prank calls. I pretended I heard the word *drums*, explained that I didn't play drums and wasn't interested. He was not an intelligent man.

My dad got a job as a commercial tractor trailer salesman that year. He made really good money and had to leave quite often to deliver rigs. He bought really nice cars, nice guns, and lots and lots of beer.

It was during his frequent overnight trips that I could have friends at the house and relax. My mom knew my friends and I were partying, and she turned a blind eye. I even took her to see the Grateful Dead on her birthday that year, and I smoked a joint right in front of her when they played *Eyes of the World*. I loved that song. She didn't say anything that night until we were almost home. She looked over me and said, "Act normal."

I think she was more paranoid than I ever was. I don't remember exactly when this happened, maybe sophomore year, but at some point my mom asked me to help her throw out all the porn. My dad must have been on an overnight delivery.

It was really bizarre handling all of that explicit material right alongside my mother. I don't remember us saying much to each other, or even making eye contact. We filled dozens of trash bags and put the bags on the curb one afternoon before the weekly trash pick up.

Some of my friends saw the bags and before long there were like fifteen kids on our front lawn digging through thousands of porn magazines. What a majorly embarrassing moment for our family. I say this must have been my sophomore year because my junior year changed everything when dad made a huge mistake.

My dad just wasn't very bright. He really wasn't. He was just a big, harsh bully. I may have been on drugs, but I was still smarter than him. I was super angry at him, too.

He went into my room one afternoon and saw an album cover he didn't like: *Aggressive Perfector* by Slayer. And he also hated all of my Grateful Dead albums, my Led Zeppelin albums, my Pink Floyd albums. Today these would be valuable collector's items.

He threw away all of my records. I wanted to fucking kill him. However, I was soon going to get my revenge another way.

One day he told me to meet him in the basement. I did. When I got to the bottom of the steps, he walked me to part of the basement near a workbench.

"I have a lot of money down here, and you will never find it," he bragged. I don't remember much else. All I know is that I immediately noticed a key hanging in a rafter not far from where we were standing—and I knew there was a safe in the basement.

The next day, I got the key down from the rafter and tried the safe. Didn't work. But then I remembered the locked drawer in an old desk. Sure enough, the key opened the drawer, which contained another key ... *to the safe*. And sure enough, there was thousands of dollars in that safe.

Now Jew Boy had plans.

Over the next few days I found out how to score an ounce of pot and a sheet of acid. And once I had that connection, I bought ounces of pot. And sheets of acid. I sold a little here and there, but I mostly smoked the pot and ate all the acid. That sheet of acid was my ticket away from reality.

You know what, though? No one needs a *sheet* of acid. And when you have as much pot and acid as I had, you tend to acquire friends. I shared freely with my friends.

Now, by this time, I'm sixteen and huge into the Grateful Dead, and I'd been to a few shows. I wore tie-dyed shirts and Guatemalan pants. I even had a dyed Mohawk. And didn't give a shit about school. I had gotten in a few fights. I had been suspended numerous times and was pretty much at risk of getting thrown out.

At some point my dad found out about the missing money. He didn't blame me—he blamed my mom. He didn't think I was smart enough to find it and I never heard them fighting about it. I just know he suspected my mother of taking that money.

He was going to find out soon that I was indeed smart enough to find it.

The school removed the smoking section that year. Too many fights and fires, and too many drugs. I would light up anyway. I was too high to care. I was actually in line for pizza in the cafeteria one day when I decided to light up a cigarette. A teacher saw me, and I bolted out of the cafeteria door. I jumped into the bushes along the outside of the building and when the teacher ran past, I ran back into the cafeteria and hid under a table. The teacher came back in and asked everyone where I took off to, and they said they didn't know.

My locker didn't have any books in it. It was full of empty Mountain Dew bottles in the bottom half, and the top half contained "Marlboro Beach." I made little people figures out of used Marlboro packs and I stole a container of Clorox from the janitor to transport and pour the sand. One of my friend's added some cocktail umbrellas. The interior of my locker was already blue, so it was actually a pretty decent diorama.

One day, the principal decided he wanted to investigate my locker. My name was called over the announcing system to report to the principal's office. To say he was shocked at what he found was an understatement. He proceeded to sniff every Mountain Dew bottle in there. I explained it was just Mountain Dew, but he insisted it was vodka because I wasn't normal. I honestly felt pretty normal that day.

I was suspended for three days.

When you're suspended, the school would send a letter home. The trick was to intercept the letter and enjoy three days of "Ferris Bueller-style" vacation. The letter arrived the first day, a Monday. I grabbed it and spent the rest of the day with a couple of friends. The next day, I convinced some friends to go hang out in a park with me and get high all day. The third day, no one wanted to cut class anymore and I couldn't stay home, so my friend offered his van in the remote parking lot at school for the day. Worked for me.

It was March and it was *cold* outside. There was some snow on the ground. The van had no heat, but I was on acid, so I either didn't notice or didn't care. But what I did notice was the gym class running around the track not far from the van.

In the back of the class was the gym teacher—not the old, senile gym teacher, but the anti-drug, religious, only-had-one-beer-in-his-life gym teacher, and I wasn't sure if he'd seen me sitting in the van's driver seat with my feet resting on the dashboard. I couldn't really go anywhere, so I just decided to play wait-and-see.

Two of my friends decided to cut lunch and hang out with me, and a cop driving past the school saw my friends getting in the van. I didn't see the cop until I was taking a hit off a joint and looked over my left shoulder to see him staring into the window right next to me.

I did the natural thing and yelled, "Duck!" And slunk down in the seat.

I'll never forget the conversation with that cop. I'll never forget any minute of the rest of that day. I was high as a fucking kite. I was on acid. And I was busted. And I will still never forget any of it. I was seventeen and this was almost thirty years ago.

The cop opened the van door and said, "You know, that's probable cause right there." Then he took my joint and bagged it. Then he called for backup and they searched the van. They found my last four doses of LSD in my jacket. At first, I claimed it wasn't my jacket, but they had seen me wearing it before. It wasn't an ordinary jacket. It was a denim jacket with acrylic paintings of Grateful Dead album covers all over it. My friend then was an amazing artist, and his painting of the *Reckoning* cover on the back of the jacket was beautiful. The whole jacket was a work of art. Wish I still had it.

That artistic friend is in prison for a double homicide now, and I'll get to that story later.

I prayed. I wasn't religious, but I found religion in that foxhole at that moment. As I sat handcuffed in the back of the police cruiser, I prayed to God to help me never end up in a situation like that again.

I was processed at the station and placed in a holding cell. Thank God I was only seventeen—I was facing drug distribution charges in a Drug-Free School Zone during the Reagan years. This was no joke.

I cannot tell you how intense it is to be on acid in a holding cell for an entire day. They kept me in there until I came down from the acid. It was incredibly intense, and not in a good way. I did not have a fun time.

Just to fuck with me, they would open the cell door every hour or so and make me bend over and spread my butt cheeks. They said they were prepping me for prison.

There was another cop in this story who offered me some encouragement. He told me he had gotten in trouble before deciding to become a cop. Today he is still a great friend of mine. He retired from the police force and became an ordained minister. He's among the most influential people in my life. He encouraged me to continue with this book. I'm still not religious, but I respect the insight of a few religious people.

Meanwhile, my dad showed up. I was let out of the cell, and *man* did I get an ass-chewing from the detective. He wanted to know where I got the acid, and I told him honestly: I'd bought it from some random dude at a Grateful Dead show. I couldn't help him. The look on my dad's face when he found out I was on acid—his whole reaction—was disbelief.

"He's totally normal," he said. This was normal then. For me.

When we got home, my dad was really fucking pissed off, and justifiably so this time. He figured out I had stolen his money. He threw me around the house for a bit, but I don't remember him hitting me. I do, however, remember my mom defending me, at least verbally. It was the first time I can remember her doing that with my dad.

I need to emphasize right now that I'm a fucking lucky person. If you are fucking lucky, you should quit while you are ahead. If you don't know if you are lucky, don't take stupid chances with your future.

One of my uncles was a cop in town, and he worked my drug bust out with the courts such that, because I was a minor, I could go to a rehab center rather than jail. I never even went before a judge.

I was expelled from school, though. I didn't have a car, but I did save up quite a bit of money since I'd been working several jobs in restaurants and gas stations after school and wasn't paying for drugs.

As restitution for stealing my dad's money, I had to pay for my own rehab, which was exactly the amount I had saved. Off I went for forty-five days of help.

I wasn't Jew Boy anymore.

CHAPTER FOUR
A SECOND CHANCE

I fucking loved rehab! I had a great time. The rehab was up in the mountains. It was almost summer, the weather was beautiful, and it wasn't a grim, lock-down facility. It was like a retreat.

I was housed in the Young Adult camp. Our group was really cool, which surprised me. There were some bad-ass kids in this group but we all got along. It was like a vacation with decaf coffee and lots of counseling. And it was really fun.

It was AIDS Awareness Week and I became Captain Condom. I took my bedsheets and some clear, plastic trash bags, and the rest of my cabin helped transform me into Captain Condom. Captain Condom was then guided through the entire camp, knocking door-to-door to announce, "Captain Condom says, 'Enclose it, don't expose it!'" Counselors were quickly called to our cabin to investigate.

I was outside the door as they came running into the cabin. I told one counselor I did it, but he just kept on telling me not to kid around. A few minutes later, that counselor came back out. He really liked me and saw a lot of potential in me. He looked at me and said, "You know? This isn't actually a bad thing; it's not like you were slamming squirrels against trees or anything." And the whole thing was dropped. However, Captain Condom became a real-life superhero for the entire center and everyone knew it was me. I gave that whole place a laugh I think we all needed.

I fucking loved rehab. Except for one thing from home: I knew that my motherfucking "dad" was cheating on my mom.

I told her before I went off to rehab that I thought he was cheating on her. No one needs to go the grocery store that often. Or go buy socks three times a week. My mom was oblivious and I think she chose to be. But then I got the phone call and I fucking blew up.

I don't remember what I was yelling, but I was yelling. Hard. I was escorted to my primary counselor's office. He was such a nice guy.

"What's wrong?"

"My mom just told me my dad's having an affair."

He called her. I'm pretty certain that he told her calling me with her news had been a bad idea. I don't think it was. I came to terms with it pretty fast, because to me, that meant their marriage was over. I was fucking overjoyed.

When the counselors realized this was good news for me, I was permitted to call my mom back. She told me her husband was dating the one female police officer in our town. My mom was devastated. I was not because his ass was moving out to be with his girlfriend, and I was coming back to a home free of him. Free of the drunkenness and names and disrespect for my mother. Just free.

About the disrespect for my mother. He treated her like shit. His nickname for her was Thunder Thighs. He'd fucking go off on her for stupid, routine shit.

He never hit her, but I remember he did grab her by the shirt collar once and cocked his fist. I was maybe four or five and sitting two feet from them on the dining room floor. I don't remember what they were fighting about—probably because they fought all of the time. And his yelling was thunderous. I know our neighbors could hear it despite having a decent space between us.

Anyway, he was moving out and it was awesome. I helped him pack his shit and move out and was thrilled to do it. I helped him get it into his apartment. This was also awesome.

That's when I got productive. There were teachers at my high school who knew I'd had it bad at home and they liked me. They offered to meet me at my grandmother's house and catch me up on as much as possible. I owe a great deal to these teachers. I earned enough credits to only have to repeat my junior year and could graduate with half days my senior year. My last two years were a breeze. I was focused, engaged, and actually wanted to learn.

I went back to high school at almost nineteen years old. I attended AA meetings. I wasn't really an alcoholic, but it was the only program I could go to every day, which was a part of the deal worked out with the judge. Instead of probation, I had to attend AA meetings for three years.

I stayed clean for more than three years. I loved AA as an organization. I loved the people in the meetings. I loved hearing the stories. I loved that I was happy without being high. The only time I got in trouble during my last two years of high school was for skipping a study hall on a Wednesday. There was an AA meeting during that time.

The principal asked me why I was cutting class. When I told him my reason, I was allowed to skip out of study hall on Wednesdays.

I was working two jobs. I bought a car. I had a checking account. My life was pretty good for perhaps the first time in my sober life. But I had issues with girls.

I was highly interested in girls and close with a few, but I never actually dated. I didn't really get that chance. I didn't trust myself, because what I knew about relationships was based on porn, and how was I going to perform with those images in my head? I was somewhat neurotic with this issue. All of these years later, I am still somewhat neurotic with this issue.

After returning to school and everyone realizing I was actually clean, I was invited to join a peer support group. Joining that group was incredible. These kids and the counselor wanted to hear my story and they asked if I would like to tell it at other high schools. I did, and I was good at it.

I went to several schools throughout the state. I was a guest speaker at my own school. Our school held a "Mental Health Day Fair." I was asked to be one of lecturers on addiction. I had a classroom all to myself for the day, with a steady audience for each lecture of about forty-five minutes. I told my story, and I talked about twelve-step programs, and how to seek help.

It was heady stuff and such a turn-around in my life then. I'm wiping tears from eyes right now as I write this.

I could speak to a crowd with confidence, but around "dad" all I could do was mumble and stutter. Turns out I have a fucking gift for teaching, and that dickhead robbed me of it for years. What a fucking asshole. Part of why I'm writing this book is to come to terms with all this shit.

Fuck, this is hard.

Anyway, a reporter from the local paper kept trying to interview me, and all day I kept declining. I'm glad I didn't do the interview. I'm glad there is no public record of me that day—I think that could have come back to haunt me at some point.

I was also invited to join anti-drug activist David Toma at an event to tell my story in front of the whole school. Shortly after these events, the group counselor nominated me for the state's Young Citizen's Award and dinner with a state senator.

Me, a model Young Citizen.

That award dinner with the senator was with all the other nominees. I wasn't the overall winner. To be honest, the nomination package the counselor sent up was careless and mistake-prone. My package was typed over the previous year's nominee, and it had words like "she" in the write-up that hadn't been changed to "he." I didn't care.

It may sound clichéd, but after everything I'd been through, it really did mean a lot just to be nominated.

I was twenty years old when I graduated high school. I was the oldest student ever to graduate from that school in a normal class, but I was treated great by everyone. I had no enemies. I was voted "Most Outrageous" for the yearbook because I made a lot of people laugh.

I actually won election as class president, but I wasn't allowed to serve because my campaign posters were considered inappropriate: "Vote for *ME* or else…" The "or else" was covered by a piece of paper that when flipped up uncovered the consequence: "I'll date your sister," and other bad options.

I also had a poster that said "69 reasons to vote for ME!" The last reason was that I didn't suck. I was awarded the position of Class Historian, which never existed until my run for office. I got screwed in the election and even the staff called bullshit, which was awesome. It didn't change anything, but these people genuinely liked me and that meant the entire world compared to my early home life.

I really enjoyed my last two years of high school. My life was pretty carefree and happy. I had overcome drugs, graduated high school with the respect of my classmates and teachers, and was looking forward to the future.

And then my "dad" came back.

At first, he came back in the afternoons to rule our house with a terror I had never seen before. By this time in his life, he was diagnosed with diabetes and could no longer drink beer. He was a raging dry alcoholic.

His relationship with the cop ended, and I have no idea why. He fucking hated me for giving my mom the idea that he was cheating. I ruined his life. I was the reason neither of his relationships had worked out. Not him. Me.

But my mom let this dude move back in and our lives would be forever changed again. He fucking hated me, but he couldn't drink that away anymore. Things got physical between us. I was grabbed, punched. The look in his eyes was that of a fucking mad man.

I didn't have enough money to move out and I was scared to try to join the military because of all the trouble I'd just been in. I felt like I had nowhere to go, so I bought beer. And I wasn't even twenty-one yet.

It was right around this time that I became "White Nigger."

CHAPTER FIVE
WHITE NIGGER

White Nigger" had a job and a car. He actually kind of had a girlfriend. He wasn't a virgin anymore, at least. But he didn't have enough money to go anywhere. So, at twenty years old, I was stuck at home. Then I wrecked my car.

I was sober when I wrecked it, but I couldn't afford another car at that moment. Pot was starting to sound good to me again. And it was. Pills started to sound good, too. And they were. And then I was partying like Jew Boy and getting abused as White Nigger. I don't remember doing a lot of acid, though. I remember eating some mushrooms once during this period.

My dad started charging me rent. My dad was still telling me to join the Army. By this point in my life, I'm like, *Fuck that! Why the fuck would I want to turn out like you?*

I eventually got another car. By then I was almost twenty-two and still living a shitty existence—and that dude would still kick my door open and just go off on me every morning.

"Get the fuck up, White Nigger! You ain't living here for free! Go chop fucking firewood!"

This was the biggest chore—chopping, stacking, and splitting firewood every morning. Oh yeah, the dude would kick my door in buck naked. And he would scream "Don't eyeball me!" So, I'm left looking off into right or left and that's not good enough either. He wanted me to watch his dick and balls jiggle while he fucking berated me. I felt so fucking broken.

It was during this time that I met the girl who would become my ex-wife. I fell in love with someone as crazy as I was, sometimes even crazier. She watched a lot of porn too, so I felt comfortable with her. I felt like we had something profound in common. She lived at home with her parents and she was a few months older than me. Again, this made me comfortable.

Her parents really loved me. My ex-wife was undiagnosed bipolar. She had fits of rage and moments of real compassion. She had never been medicated, and just like me treated her troubles with pot and other drugs. Her mom called me a saint. Her dad said I needed to find a real job. He wanted her to start her own life and wanted me to play a part in it.

We started saving money together, but we were also partying every day. At that rate, we were never going to get out of where we were, which I don't think really bothered her, but it really bothered me. I needed to get the hell out of there.

I ran away a few times in high school, but only for a couple days. I think the longest was like four days and I took shelter at a friend's parent's house.

One night, I wrote a note stating I was running away for good. I didn't go very far. I ran away to a foster home in my town where there was a girl there I really liked. We got drunk. I'd passed out after drinking with all the kids in the house. I was woken up by my dad, who dragged me out of that house by my hair. He punched me in the face. Threw me around the house when we got home. That beatdown was really bad. I had a fat lip.

It was so bad I pretended I was crazy. I totally pretended to be insane. I started chanting lyrics to Metallica (*Sanitarium*) and Slayer (*Angel of Death*). I scared my younger brother so bad he ran screaming when he heard me. I put on a fucking good act. So good that the beatings stopped, and I saw a psychologist for a few weeks.

I think the psychologist figured out my real story, so he corroborated it in that I had been sleepwalking, wrote the note that I was running away while sleepwalking and partied with those other kids while sleepwalking.

My mom knew it was all bullshit, and my dad really thought I was losing my mind. That first probable sleepwalking episode in my dad's bedroom gave my story some real credibility.

I had to drop that aside in here to try and help explain why I didn't just pack up and leave that house. Leaving had never worked before, and without a real plan, it wouldn't work again.

I was starting to get desperate to leave and I was seeing very little hope of getting out of there. I started thinking about killing myself. And White Nigger almost did, but he didn't because of a commercial.

He called the suicide intervention crisis line instead.

Phone calls weren't able to be traced so easily back in early 1990s, unlike how they can today. I didn't give my street address and didn't want to, but I wanted help. I had all the weapons and ammunition to kill a community but I didn't want to die, and I didn't want the cops at my parent's house either.

After I assured him I wouldn't kill myself that night, the counselor on the phone told me to report to the local hospital the next morning. He said I needed to go that hospital and go to "Skip." I told him that I would see Skip in the morning.

I had never been in a hospital before except for when my grandmother was treated for a brain tumor. When I walked up to the nurse at the entrance and said I wanted to see Skip, I was surprised at how fast I got introduced. Skip wasn't a person, Skip was SCIP.

I was escorted to the Suicide Crisis Intervention Program.

CHAPTER SIX
MY THIRD CHANCE

I never did return home. I was finally out of that house. In fact, I wasn't *allowed* back to the house because of all the guns. Also, I wasn't allowed back in the house because my dad was pissed that I told the hospital about all the guns.

Following a few days in the SCIP, I was released to a state halfway house. My future ex-wife visited me often. She understood my problems. She supported me. She saw potential in me that I didn't see in myself.

I was finally able to call work and explain what happened. I was allowed to keep my job. This was huge because, by this time, I had a decent truck and enough money for at least a small apartment.

The apartment was a shithole. I shared a four-bedroom, one-bathroom house with three other tenants. My room was enough for a TV, a bed, a small fridge, and dresser. And that's all I had. The other tenants were not doing as well. One man was elderly and deaf. One man was an alcoholic epileptic who didn't take his meds. And lastly, the landlord's resident underling was psychotic. He knocked on my door once, held a pubic hair to my face, and asked if it belonged to me because it was left on the toilet seat. He was not normal.

This was home for about six months, and my future ex-wife stayed there with me. Then, one morning, my truck died and I couldn't make it work—and something might have snapped in me.

This was no way to live. This was not going to be my existence. It had been five years since I was arrested, and I was pretty certain I didn't have a criminal record.

I was going to join the Navy.

CHAPTER SEVEN
IN THE NAVY

The Navy gave me something I never, ever had before—*respect*. All those years being groomed for the Army paid off huge when I joined the Navy. All of those times I had my "dad"—that fucked-up, drill-sergeant wannabe—calling me Alice and Jew Boy and White Nigger. Fuck, man. I had already been broken once, so the service couldn't do anything worse. I belonged in the Navy. I fucking loved the Navy. The Navy saved me.

So fuck you, Dad—and fuck the Army.

Navy Boot Camp was easy. It took me a few times to get the marching orders down, but I was placed in charge as the Recruit Chief Petty Officer over the other eighty recruits in my division. I was a fucking leader. And, oh my God, I was a good one.

Those recruits hardly ever gave me a problem. I didn't yell very often at anyone, but when I did, I was scarier than the company commanders (CC, the two senior Sailors who were actually in charge of us). When I wasn't yelling, I was telling jokes and making people laugh. Even one of the hard-ass CCs.

We had marched somewhere in the compound where the CC stopped us to tell us some soldiers had died in a used Turkish plane the Army was using for some mission. I didn't mean to say it loud, but I said, "The moral to that story is to stay away from leftover Turkey." The CC laughed, and I was on easy street for the rest of my time in boot camp. I fucking loved boot camp.

The only problem I had there was with the job I was going to have after graduating. I joined the Navy to be an Operations Specialist. At the time, it was a job that opened the door to becoming a SEAL, which is exactly what I wanted to be. I didn't expect something called the Moment of Truth.

Moment of Truth occurs the second or third day of boot camp. An investigative agent was introduced to us. He said that if we didn't come clean about everything in our past or if we lied about anything when we joined, we were facing tens of thousands of dollars in fines and up to ten years in jail.

I didn't just raise my hand, I stood up.

The guy looked surprised. That scared me. I was in a fucking panic when I was led away to a tiny room to meet with a Sailor who asked what I did. I sat down, I said, "I never went to court to for this, but I was busted with acid, thrown out of school, went to rehab, went back to school, and lied my ass off about all of this."

He said, "You never went to court?" I said no. He said, "Dude, you're stupid for standing here." But because it was possibly in my high school records, he put *LSD (x2)* (which means I did acid twice) in my record.

A few days later, I was called into our company commanders' office, and they were pissed. They couldn't believe that I came clean like that because the Navy would have never found out. They really liked me, and they were worried I now wasn't going to get the Navy job I wanted.

I had won awards in boot camp. I won the overall leadership award over every Sailor in my class, which was about a thousand other recruits. Those were great mood enhancers for me, especially considering what I left behind back home, but the last day of boot camp was a crusher.

I was called to a room and met with a young Sailor who sat me down and said bluntly, "Look man, you're not going to be an Operations Specialist." They didn't like that I had lied about doing acid.

He asked me if I could type. I said no.

He said, "Well, here's the deal. Your company commanders really like you. I have a job open for a journalist. Do you want it? You have to pass a typing test."

What if I don't pass?

"Then you don't get a job—and trust me, you don't want to leave here without a job."

I took the typing test. I had used a typewriter before, but never one without a correction button. This one did not have a correction button.

That Sailor set the timer, and I set off to typing. The bell rang at five minutes and I handed him my typing test.

"Try again," he said.

And then again.

Finally, he said, "I'm going to go smoke. When I get back, I'm going to start the timer. In the meantime, you keep typing."

I did the best I could. He looked over the paper, looked at me, and smiled.

"Sixteen words a minute. You can type better than me. You're going to be a journalist."

CHAPTER EIGHT
THE NAVY JOURNALIST

My journalism school was *fucking hard*. I had never had an interest in actually being a journalist, Navy or civilian, but I didn't want to fail out of journalism school and not have a job.

My future ex-wife and I were still together, and she wanted to get married. She only lived two hours away. The training took six months, so she would visit me on weekends and the relationship seemed to be going okay.

We eloped while I attended J-school. She didn't tell her parents and I didn't tell mine. We got married because I thought I could get an assignment to a ship just a few states away and she could be relatively close to her family; she had never lived away from her parents. If I had remained single, my first tour was going to be in Bahrain, which I had never heard of—and I'd be there for two years without her. I got the orders to the ship. We had a wedding planned for the family later that year after I graduated.

I barely made it through school. The first half was print journalism, public affairs (public relations), and photography. I had no passion for photography. I had little interest in finding news stories. Desktop publishing was still an emerging technology, but that's what I was trained on. I was trained with the first version of Photoshop and Adobe PageMaker.

This is where I had my fun—in print journalism. To learn the software, we were encouraged to just fool around with it. So, I started making a fake newspaper with stories about people who could target-shoot by farting BBs and other such bullshit. It was awesome. I didn't really care a lot for the public affairs stuff, and I had to retake a few tests in that area to get through.

The next three months was broadcast journalism. I had very little passion for that at the start, but once I caught on, I had a lot of fun with it. These weren't the skills I had expected from a military career, but at least I was learning something.

Yes, I said *career*. I was not going to be my dad. I was not going to get out after a few years and regret not staying until I was eligible for a pension. I signed on for the long haul. And journalism challenged my determination to reach this goal.

I arrived at my first ship, an aircraft carrier that was under construction. I was the first journalist to arrive to that ship. My job was to work with my young public affairs officer to start building our public affairs office, establish the on-board radio and television stations, start putting together the ship's newsletters, and help the photo lab when necessary. It was a huge job and much of it was completely new to me. I hardly ever saw my future ex-wife during this tour. However, I did spend some time with my mother's first husband and his family during this tour.

It was surreal to receive a letter on the ship from someone with the same last name as me. It was a letter from my mother's first husband's father, and he and his wife and son wanted to meet me. I agreed. I took a week of leave and flew to meet part of my history. It was fucking weird. The whole trip was fucking weird.

My mom's first husband met me at the airport. I towered over this guy. He looked kind of like Danny DeVito. I was about twenty-five when we met. I didn't look anything like this guy. It only got stranger from here.

He picked me up at the airport in his BMW, which he drove while wearing leather driving gloves and a British "flat hat." He drove us to his house, an old, abandoned but refurbished railroad hub center. He lived in a remote location and this building was as small as a single-car garage. It was loaded with books from floor to ceiling.

We entered his house and he immediately went to the kitchen, emerging with a large carving knife that he waved around for a few seconds with a really bizarre, almost savage look in his eyes, and then announced we were having elk heart for dinner. I was relieved to find out I was living long enough to have dinner. Elk heart is delicious.

After dinner he sparked a joint. It hurts to write this, but I took a hit. This goes against so many military values and regulation. I did it partially because I had a sense of obligation, partially because I was guest there, but mostly because a moment to smoke with this mysterious part of my personal history was a once-in-a-lifetime opportunity.

The next day we drove more than an hour to meet his parents in a wealthy community. It was summer and this town was beautiful. His dad was a retired WWII fighter pilot and a genius. He taught himself to speak English just before joining the Navy from the French Quarter in New Orleans. He joined as an enlisted Sailor and earned pilot wings as a petty officer, later retiring as a commander.

He read books about construction and built his first house by hand. My mom's hippie-child first husband was also a genius, but I'm pretty certain he was the borderline-insane kind. He was Harvard educated, but adopted music as his passion. Like I mentioned, he had been my mom's piano teacher. By the time I met him, he was a private violin teacher.

His dad had a sailing yacht, and that's where we spent the next two or three days. This was about twenty years ago so I don't remember all of the details. The whole situation was too uncomfortable, awkward, and bizarre: I honestly regret making that trip. They wanted to believe I was family, tried convincing themselves that I was family.

Tried really hard, in fact. His mom said there were tall people in her family and that's where I got my height. I was like Gulliver in the land of the Little People. This was not family. And I was trapped on their fucking yacht.

The only event I remember in full detail was at sunset on our first night of sail, when his dad grabbed a set of church choir bells. It turned out he was a bell ringer at his church. And not just any bell ringer, he was proud to announce he was the *best* bell ringer. His son took out his violin. I don't remember if his mom had an instrument, but I do remember being handed a triangle, the metal kind with the little wand. And then the music started.

The bells were ringing, the violin was playing, and at odd intervals came the ding of that stupid triangle. It was very awkward and their words of encouragement weren't helping.

Ding.

I felt like the kid at a party who was only invited because the school said everyone had to be included.

Ding.

They lived far enough north that even during the height of summer seals swam alongside the yacht. This was not a deterrent to swimming. Late the next morning, I said I was going for a swim off the side of the boat. They thought I was crazy but didn't try to stop me. I dove into the water and swam. I could see a town from the yacht. I was swimming to that town. I have no idea how far I swam, but I made it.

The town had an ice-cream shop and I needed some alone time. I was cold, wet, and had a few wet dollars in my pocket. I ordered a banana split and enjoyed my alone time.

The boat docked some time later. His mother called me tenacious, and I think they started to understand how I was really feeling. We sailed back to their town. I don't remember much else of the visit. I just remember how badly I wanted to leave.

I never heard from them again. And I'm fine with that.

After returning to the ship, I focused on my new trade. I started becoming quite good at journalism. I started writing articles about the crew and the ship's progress and doing video work for safety training videos. I stayed on with that ship for an additional year, for a total of five years. I asked for the additional year so I didn't miss the maiden deployment.

I loved that ship, I loved the crew, and I loved being a Sailor. I loved being a shipboard firefighter. I loved doing maintenance on the systems our division was responsible for. And I served on that ship with some amazing people. One of the best was a female master chief.

She was fucking fiery. The Navy had just started to allow females to serve on surface combatant vessels. I would have served with her in the bowels of Hell. She was just fucking cool. Thank God she had a sense of humor.

Sunday routine at sea on that ship was pretty lax. Our new department head was not lax. He had just reported aboard during deployment and he wanted Sunday to be just like any other day at sea, but our master chief looked out for us. She told us one morning, "Sundays are going to be regular work days from now on. However, you can all attend church *wink-wink*. After you all attend 'church' you can come to work."

That Sunday, we all slept in until noon. The department head said we didn't attend church services and he came down hard on that master chief that tried to give us a break.

The next Sunday, we were all called to muster with her.

"You guys really screwed me on that church thing. I mean you guys *really* screwed me on that church thing..."

I didn't realize how loud I said it, but the words *It's called a pew* came out of my mouth. Holy fuck—what was I thinking? I thought I was dead man.

All the chiefs were dying laughing, all of the Sailors were fucking laughing. And I got called to stand with the master chief.

Fuck, this can't be good.

She said, "That was funny."

And that was it. She was fucking awesome. I loved that crew.

I really loved my job as a journalist. In fact, I liked it so much and was good enough at it that I asked to become a journalism instructor at the school for my next tour.

I was a really good Sailor. I climbed the enlisted ranks unbelievably fast during that tour. I went from seaman apprentice to petty officer 1st class in that five-year timeframe. That was almost unheard of but became possible due to changes in the promotion system. I had stellar evaluations, which shortened my waiting time to take promotion exams. I earned three Navy and Marine Corps Achievement Medals (NAMs) during that tour. I had taken a lot of additional responsibilities and was considered an overachiever, and the NAMs earned me a new nickname with the crew—"Nambo." That nickname still makes me laugh.

While I was working on the ship and going out to sea, my future ex-wife was busy with a horse we bought. We lived in really cheap housing and I was making the best money I had ever made in my life, though that's a relative amount: I wasn't making all that much. She started working in a tack shop and found a discarded race horse for sale for only a few thousand dollars, so we bought a horse.

Long story short, the horse died after a fall. My wife was devastated because she had been riding the horse at the time. Another long story short: I hated that horse. She spent all of our money on that damned thing and didn't tell me first. Finding out this fact was the beginning of the end of our marriage.

The ship was about halfway through deployment when I got the message regarding my request to be an instructor at the journalism school: "Thank you for shopping," it read, and I was off to be a journalism instructor.

The move made much easier by not having a fucking horse.

The journalism school was only two hours from where I grew up, and I went home to visit once in a while. The first time I showed up my "dad" was a whole different person. I wasn't Alice or Jew Boy or White Nigger anymore—I was "Admiral." He was beyond happy that I had joined the military. It was like part of his life's dream came true. I was out of the house, and in the military. I think he was also beyond happy because about this time he discovered the magic of opioid painkillers. I was happy because I'd never live in that house ever again.

I didn't visit very often. We had very little of any real substance to discuss, and my family had more wreckage than ever.

The first time I came home to visit, I went upstairs to see my middle brother. He was detoxing from heroin. I'll never forget how wretched he looked. My youngest brother, who I hardly knew at all, occupied a bedroom filled with cigarette butts. He had burned holes in his bedpost with cigarettes. I didn't really see much of my sister. She was off with her future ex-husband.

I was close with my sister and her husband for a few years. I would actually come home just to visit with them. They had it really good for several years. Then things got way fucked up. I'll talk about this more later.

My marriage was starting to become a bigger wreck too. My wife was unable to assimilate to the military lifestyle. It isn't for everybody, it's true, and it just was not for her.

There were times I thought we were going to physically fight. She had always had a mean streak, but there was just something really wrong with her during our time with the journalism school.

It was drugs.

She was using drugs all the time when I was away on the ship. I had no idea because I was hardly ever around. We didn't live on a base when I was on the ship, but in the journalism school tour, we lived on the base where the school is located. The journalism school is near Washington, DC and Annapolis, and adjacent to the ultra-secret National Security Agency.

The base was under the highest security levels at that time because the terror attacks of 9/11 happened a week before I arrived to begin my new job. Cars were being all but dismantled as they entered the base, and it could take up to two hours to get through the gate.

I voluntarily stood duty as gate guard over the Christmas holiday two-week "stand down," which is basically when everyone is authorized to take paid leave. The gates were still in high alert. Gate duty was hard duty during that time. It was twelve-hour shifts in the middle of December and we were dismantling cars, taking out seats, pulling apart door panels—but not every car. There was a justifiable random pattern, but I'm not going to disclose what that was.

Anyway, living on base made getting to work really easy. Getting drugs? Not so much. She didn't have the ability to get her drugs without risking some serious consequences.

After about a year on base, the security excitement at the gate settled down a bit and my wife got a job at the local horse-racing track. She was an exercise rider, warming up the horses before races.

She made good money and blew it on dope. With security becoming less tight on base, she asked a friend from back home to start mailing drugs to her.

Sending drugs through the mail to a military base was nothing I wanted to be associated with. The last straw was the day I found drugs inside a VHS videotape that was mailed to our house.

Our marriage was over and it couldn't be over fast enough. The law for that state was a mandatory year of separation before the divorce could be officially granted.

It was during our separation that I started gaining more confidence with women, and I started dating. My dating experience wasn't all that great, so the phone call from a U.S. Army Sergeant 1st Class asking if I could speak Arabic, which I answered with a "no" and he answered back with "that's okay, you're going to Iraq," was welcomed news. I was actually really happy to get that phone call.

I was off to Iraq.

CHAPTER NINE
THE SANDBOX

The journalism school's leadership thought highly enough of me to choose me as a team member for the school's first-ever mobile training team sent to a combat zone. I was off to train members of the Iraqi government how to operate with a free press in a (hopefully) democratic society—something none of these people were familiar with.

I was going to do something my dad didn't do. I was going to be boots on the ground in a war zone, deploying with a mix of six staff from Army, Marines, and Air Force. I was the only Sailor.

It was 2004, and there was quite a bit going on—personally and with *Operation Iraqi Freedom*. My divorce was final the day my foot touched Iraqi sand. I was happy.

It was also the day Paul Bremmer left. There was a bounty on his head, and the Green Zone, the huge fortified coalition headquarters compound, was pretty tense that day. It didn't matter to me. I was as far away as I had ever been from where I grew up and the terrible memories associated with it. I had a real mission. I experienced incoming mortars, rockets, and small-arms fire. I experienced a car bomb blast. But none of that compares to what I experienced with the Iraqi people.

My first meal in Baghdad was inside one of Saddam's opulent palaces. The place was amazing. The detail in the tiling, the overall architecture, was just stunning.

I ate alone. The Army officer in charge of our team and I didn't get along because he was a lot like my dad. I started thinking the Army was just full of assholes—which isn't true—but it seemed that way when he started calling me names.

He called me Gilligan, and would slap my head with this hat just like in the old TV show. I finally had enough one day and went off on him. I was surprised to find he actually respected me after that.

Makes me wonder what would have happened if I ever went off on my dad. It doesn't matter now.

I ate alone until three Iraqis approached my table, set their food down and joined me. I was beyond freaked out. It's against regulations to have a loaded firearm in a dining area unless you are with security, but my first thoughts were how fast can I lock and load in my current situation.

They were in traditional garb, the two females completely shielded from view behind their hijabs and burkas. The male was wearing the robe-like garment.

I was doing everything in my power to not make eye contact. I just looked around the palace and focused on the intricate tiles. I have no idea how the females ate while veiled because I was desperately ignoring them. But I certainly understand English when I hear it.

"It's beautiful, isn't it?" commented the younger of the two women about our palatial surroundings. Nearly speechless, I could only reply with a *Yes, it is.*

They introduced themselves as a family just arrived back from the United States, where their daughter had graduated medical school. All three of them were doctors. And all three of them were a family. I had never had a conversation with anyone who looked like them before. I knew my students would look like them, but that was a classroom. This was different.

They were very nice people and we had a very pleasant conversation. They were not at all what I thought they would be like. That was just the first of many such epiphanies during my time with the

Iraqi people.

Our Iraqi students risked their very lives every day just to attend our classes, which consisted of everything from the fundamentals of democracy to how to use Photoshop. We held mock press conferences and did mock television interviews. The goal was to teach them to generate positive public messages in their own language and to get away from U.S. military faces explaining Iraqi issues.

At the core, the students wanted what I wanted—a free and independent Iraq. I honestly believed strongly in this mission. They honestly believed in our team. It's humbling to revisit all of this again.

They liked us enough to warn us about upcoming "holidays." It took us a while to catch on to sudden announcements of "tomorrow's a holiday." But there was a pattern here. Something bad happened on every holiday. The car bomb I mentioned earlier? That took place at the gate right outside of our classrooms. I sure am glad we were on a holiday.

I'm *really* glad our students liked us.

I honestly don't know if our team was successful in our mission. I'll probably never know. Iraq turned into a real shit show since my time there. I'm hopeful, but I'm doubtful.

We had an Iraqi colonel in one of our courses. Graduation day, he stood up from his chair, walked over to me and called me a *dick*.

"You're a *dick*. A great, big *dick!*" he exclaimed as he shook my hand. The major in charge of our team immediately agreed. I was confused. Then another student approached the colonel, whispered in his ear, and the colonel turned a bright shade of red.

In Arabic, *dik* means rooster. Iraqis hold roosters in high regard for their bravery and fighting abilities—it's a term of respect. So, he thought I was a *dik*.

I accepted his compliment and we hugged. An American wearing a sidearm was hugged by an unarmed Iraqi officer in a surreal moment of genuine mutual respect.

We are all human beings.

Our Iraqi translator invited our team to his home for dinner. It was a massive spread. I have no idea what we ate, but it was very good. The coalition forces had bombed his first home—destroyed all of his family's belongings—yet here he was feeding us. We did rid his country of a terrible dictator, so it didn't matter to him that his home was destroyed in the process. He was still happy to play a part in our mission, and his service was invaluable to us as well as his country.

Our students came from every religious background and they worked together in a harmony undreamt of by most media reports. They held conversations. They laughed. Every preconceived bias I held toward the Iraqi people vanished during my time there.

These people begged me to help them get to America. I wish I could have helped them do that. These are wonderful people. We have since made a real mess out of that country. It eats at me every day that the cradle of all civilization is pierced with bullet holes, pockmarked from bombs, and stained with blood.

I'm proud of my service in Iraq, regardless of the original reasons for it. Returning from there was also the end of my time at the journalism school. It was time to look for orders and I really wanted another ship.

I got orders to NATO.

Fuck.

CHAPTER TEN
NATO

During my tour with the journalism school, aside from the Iraq deployment, I had been invited to participate in NATO's *Exercise Northern Lights* as a public information specialist. This exercise took place in 2003 in Scotland and was so poorly executed the Scottish newspapers called it "Northern Debacle." They could not have been more accurate.

I will spare a lot detail here, but it was so bad, we had contests to see who could get inside our secure compound with the strangest object as identification. So far, the winner was a British officer who was able to gain access by holding up a jelly donut.

This was going to be hard to beat, but not impossible.

We had a Marine sergeant on our team who got us into the compound without any identification at all. The Czech Republic security guards were clueless. We rolled up to the gate in our tiny Renault hatchback packed with five large U.S. military members. The Marine was driving.

As he had been instructed to do, the gate guard read in English what was written on the palm of his hand.

"Are you part of the exercise?"

The Marine answered, "I have a lobster in my pants."

The guard replied, "Yah?"

The Marine replied, "Yah."

The protocol satisfied, into the compound we went.

This story basically summarizes that entire exercise and pretty much my entire view of NATO and its multinational problems.

The officer in charge of us liked me at first. I don't know if he had anything to do with my orders to NATO, but one thing was certain: He grew to dislike me before I left.

I hated working for NATO. I hated going to work every day. I hated every minute I spent with that organization though I had an amazing job. My job was to travel all over the world and report on high-level, multinational conferences and meetings.

I most often traveled alone. I loved the travel. I loved my nights in the bars all over the world. I loved NATO when I wasn't working. I hated NATO when I was.

I have most often compared NATO to the trees in *Lord of the Rings*—slow, with the potential to be powerful. The problem is NATO has a hard time being powerful and finds it much easier to be drunk and dysfunctional. I fit right in during my time there.

I drank more during that tour than at any other time in my life. Just think about that, as I often have, compared to earlier stages of my life. Alcohol is part of NATO's culture. There were two bars in the building I worked in and they were open all day. If you had access to the building, you had access to the bars. There were people who spent more time in the bars than working.

I risked becoming one of those people because I had so easily been one of them before. I needed to leave that organization. I got in trouble for the first and only time in my career during that tour.

I failed to show for a watch. I had swapped the duty schedule with someone else and I forgot because the reminder I created was on my desk. My office was under renovation, and my desk was dismantled. A few weeks had passed since we agreed to the swap, and I totally forgot about the swap.

I was at a bar, and I closed that bar. I left my phone charging back at my apartment that night. I saw all of the missed calls and voice messages when I got home. And I was loaded.

I was three hours late for an eight-hour watch by the time I drove to the headquarters. I apologized to the Sailors who were filling my position. I sent a message to everyone involved to explain how sorry I was for this error. And man, this is where journalism training comes in handy: My message was awesome, even when I read it again after sobering up. It was part of the reason the punitive administrative actions I faced were dropped.

I had to sit for a non-judicial Disciplinary Review Board (DRB) for my actions; it sounds a lot more benign than it is, because any really serious punishment could derail the Navy career I'd been working for. While the charges against me were dismissed, I was still assigned—and well deservedly so—a series of additional watches that I stood proudly.

In hindsight, I should have just stayed home that night. Driving drunk to get back and make up for the scheduling mistake I'd made was far more stupid than my original mistake. I'm lucky I didn't kill myself, or anyone else. But the universe works in strange and wondrous ways.

Two weeks later, the Navy announced I was selected for promotion to chief petty officer. I was in for a shitty couple of months.

I'll talk more about what it means to be a CPO in the next chapter, but I have another quick story to tell here, because NATO did come with some really great stories.

For example, I once stole an admiral's car. Misappropriated, really, is a better description.

I had just landed in Skopje, Macedonia from an event at Incirlik Air Base in Turkey. Prior to my trip, I was asked to plan to attend a formal dinner within an hour after my scheduled arrival. I declined the invitation. I would need time to unpack, get all of my gear in order, put on a suit ... *no, thanks.* The officer I directly reported to was a Canadian navy commander, and he agreed with my decision. I was not to attend the formal dinner in Skopje.

There was a knock on my hotel door not even thirty minutes after my check-in. I answered the door to a Norwegian Sailor who said a photographer was needed in the lobby. I asked why a photographer was needed in the lobby. He explained there was a driver waiting to take me to the formal dinner to take photos.

I hadn't even unpacked my gear from Turkey yet. I didn't bring a civilian suit, but I had a set of wrinkled Service Dress Blues (our formal Navy uniform) I could wear. I was not very thrilled.

About fifteen minutes later I met the driver in my wrinkled uniform, camera in hand. And now I'm on my way. As we left the hotel, I asked if there was food at this event. The driver explained I had missed dinner.

I asked, "How far away is this event?" The driver said it was almost an hour away.

Now I'm angry. Highly agitated. I had been cleared not to go to this event for this very reason.

Fuck this nonsense.

We arrived at the event. I all but kicked in the door to this place. I took three pictures of nothing in particular, and then walked out. The president of Macedonia was at this dinner. I didn't give a shit. The four-star U.S. Air Force general in charge of my command was also at this dinner. I still didn't give a shit. I was fucking pissed off. I fucking hated NATO just because of bullshit like this.

I was fucking hungry, tired as hell, and the command's protocol officer wanted to show off what kind of power he had by ordering me to the event. I think he noted my demeanor and immediately regretted his decision. I didn't speak to that officer the rest of my time at the command.

I was about to get back in the car and head back to my hotel when a good friend of mine, a Dutch Army warrant officer, grabbed me by the arm. He said he would get me food and booze. That was enough to change my mind and I walked back in.

My immediate boss waved me over to his table and said, "I didn't think you were going to be here." This just made me angrier because this meant the protocol officer went over my boss's head to get me there.

My boss asked me not to look so angry. I tried. I was given some food and that didn't help much. It was the kneecap of whatever animal they had for dinner. There was barely any meat on it. More importantly, though, they gave me wine.

I drank four bottles.

I took photos of everything after that. I took photos of the gift exchange between our general and the Macedonian president. I took pics of everyone at every table. I never did one fucking thing with any of those photos. No one ever asked what I did with them. I could have put them up on the command's web page. Chances are you never visited that command's web page. No one else, either.

This was NATO, so nobody cared.

Anyway, everyone knew that I had more than my fair share of wine by this point, and it was finally time to go. I found the driver who picked me up and out we went. My buddy from the Netherlands joined us. Our driver either thought I had the biggest balls on the planet or I was really high up in rank to behave the way I did without consequence. Or maybe, he thought my Dutch friend was my personal protocol officer.

The car I was escorted to was a limo.

It was not the same car that had delivered me.

My Dutch buddy grabbed me by the arm and said, "Keep your mouth shut. He thinks you're an officer. Let me open the car door for you."

So now my buddy really *was* my protocol officer. We got in the car and waited for a few minutes. Then I saw the general in charge of my command get in the car in front of us.

Police lights came on from behind our car and in front of the general's car—*I was in the British Navy admiral's limo.*

This admiral was the number-two officer in charge of the command and I had just hijacked his car.

The streets were lined with armed guards as we made our way back to the hotel. When we arrived my buddy told me to stay in the car. Our general got out of his car and entered the hotel. I then got out of my car and did the same.

No one ever said a fucking word to me about that night, and I demonstrated why it's not cool to piss off a chief petty officer.

CHAPTER ELEVEN
HAIL TO THE CHIEF

Promotion to U.S. Navy Chief Petty Officer changes everything about enlisted Sailors' careers, in their personal lives and beyond, including post-service employment. This coveted promotion is a singular, life-changing event. "Chiefs run the Navy" is how the Department of the Navy has viewed chief petty officers since the rank was created in 1893.

My mom and dad were at my pinning ceremony, where they affixed one of my anchors to my collar on one side. I wanted family to be there, and though we had a checkered and sometimes violent past, they were all I had. My other anchor was tended to by two highly influential chiefs who had greatly impacted me during my Navy career—one I was less than ten years into at that point.

I was the only Sailor selected for chief petty officer in my command. The command's Sailor of the Year was not selected. The Sailor who just went in front of a DRB two weeks ago *was* selected. This was not a good situation for anyone, least of all the spanking new chief selectee.

Me.

Chiefs train new chiefs. Chiefs train everyone. Once you're selected for advancement, you go through an Initiation process. It's intended to be hard. It challenges every aspect of your being. It's a much harder process when all the chiefs at your command don't like you.

My colleagues well knew that my attitude toward NATO was negative. Many of them saw me as unprofessional. During this tour, I often saw *myself* as unprofessional. I had a lot to prove to everyone.

What I experienced during my Initiation was the best lesson of my life. What I experienced was different than most selectees that cycle because I was the only new chief in my command—so I had the full attention of every CPO in my building.

This was good and this was bad.

I was humiliated. I was ridiculed. I was insulted. I was embarrassed. And then I was rebuilt. The times when those chiefs shunned me or threatened me or ridiculed me hurt far worse than when my dad had done it, but I felt like I deserved that treatment from people I respected, whom I wanted to respect me, and I'd fucked up before them. I didn't deserve the ridicule I suffered growing up, but I owned this one.

Those lessons will never leave me. Those lessons continued well past Initiation. Those lessons have made me who I am today. "Once a Chief, always a Chief" is not just a slogan. It's a forecast. It's a promise. It's a way of life.

But I was now a chief in a command that I was absolutely disgusted with and I couldn't wait to get away from it. Then I finally got my wish, but you know the old phrase, *Be careful what you wish for; you might get it.* I got my wish and was allowed to transfer early.

I was going to the worst ship in the United States Navy.

CHAPTER TWELVE
THE WORST SHIP IN THE FLEET

It was *really* bad there. When I arrived, morale was so low that chiefs—the backbone of the Navy!—were going AWOL. Officers were getting fired. Sailors were getting arrested out in town and getting kicked out of the Navy in well-above-normal separation numbers. And yet I was excited because I had small shoes to fill. I was going to shine. I was going to go back to be a Sailor at sea, and this time, as a *chief petty officer* at sea. I was off to a fresh start.

I set out knowing that I could make a positive impact at this command. While my official job title was Chief Mass Communication Specialist, my job on this ship was to become the Media Department Leading Chief Petty Officer, leading a section of twenty-eight Sailors. This is an incredibly small department on an aircraft carrier, but it was the perfect situation for me.

By this point in my career, I really didn't want to be a journalist or mass communication specialist anymore. As the chief running a department, I could just be a chief, a manager running the operation. And that's exactly what I became. I wasn't known by my job specialty as much as I was known to just be The Chief.

The Sailors in my department were in just as bad a shape as the rest of the ship. The chief I replaced had basically quit in frustration or fatigue. My Sailors were not qualified for watches or firefighting. They didn't belong to any emergency response stations on the ship. They only took pictures, made newsletters, made video productions, performed VIP tours, ran a radio and TV station, and ran a print shop.

They were basically civilian public relations people in Navy uniforms. The only tactical support this department performed was processing intelligence imagery and printing Secret material. Re-Sailorizing my people was the first challenge.

I was not well received. I had spoken to the chief I was supposed to work for before I arrived, and I asked about the crew. He told me they weren't standing watches. I totally disagreed with his philosophy and told him my plans to change that. So he told the Sailors before my arrival that I was going to make them act like actual Sailors. They were going to stand watches just like every other Sailor on board.

Chiefs aren't supposed to sandbag other chiefs like that and I wasn't very happy with him. I was poisoned to the Sailors before I ever set foot in the workspace.

Matters turned out differently, though, as it happened. He asked me to sit in for him at a Department Chiefs meeting. The big discussion was about problems filling the ship's watchbill. I interjected to say I would offer up my Sailors to stand watches. Unsurprisingly, the offer was instantly accepted.

I walked out of the meeting, and about ten minutes later, the chief I would be replacing was filling out his transfer paperwork. He was a rank above me and been in the Navy twice as long as I had. I think he was just tired.

Over time, things in the department improved. My Sailors started understanding the reasoning behind my decisions. Things on the ship improved, too.

A daily event called Cleaning Stations is called away for one hour each day, and Sweepers, which is fleet-wide, is called away four times a day as a fifteen to thirty-minute quick clean. Neither of these had ever been taken seriously.

The ship was fucking filthy.

A carrier is so large it has its own TV station, and I owned ours. I asked one of my Sailors to set up a camera, I grabbed a guitar (I only know a few chords) and recorded a stupid little song about cleaning the ship. It was thirty seconds long and we played the video of me singing it over the TV system whenever Sweepers was called into action. The ship's captain liked the song so much, it was played over the ship's announcing system four times a day as well. It was a hit.

People were singing along, and cleaning. Soon, other people wanted to record their own videos and songs. So, we started recording a bunch of them.

I'm not going to say I single-handedly changed the culture of an aircraft carrier, but I'm proud to look back and know I played my part—*which is what a chief does*. I also qualified to drive that ship on that assignment, and I stood the watch as Conning Officer for almost three years. I loved that tour.

But I pissed someone off I shouldn't have.

Just as I was ready to transfer from that ship, social media was beginning to really take off. I put some stuff out there that was met with disapproval from some of the senior leadership in my career field—a career field in which I had a top nomination for a senior leadership position of my own.

My behavior online prompted the highest enlisted Sailor in our field to call me on the ship to inform me personally that she had ripped up my nomination package.

I extended on the ship for an additional year, made another deployment—and wound up with a better position than what I had previously hoped for.

CHAPTER THIRTEEN
AMAZING TOURS

So much of success in life is dependent on the luck of the draw. I drew well when I fell into the Navy's world of adult learning.

I fell into the field of organizational psychology. I fell into the field of adaptive learning. I fell into the field of social sciences. I found my calling in the world of Navy training and military education. I found myself set up for success beyond the military, which I didn't really see at the time.

I met my new wife during my first tour ashore after the carrier. I had promised myself that I was never getting married again, and well, I met her through a well-known online dating site and we were married a year later. She knows my story, and I love her dearly for her understanding and boundless patience with me.

Because of how I was raised, I promised myself I would never have children. I was afraid to have children. Today I have two wonderful daughters. They aren't mine by blood, but I faced my biggest fear allowing kids into my life and *I didn't become my dad*. I resent him more now than ever before, because I have two daughters who are not afraid of me—who trust me, and willingly spend time with me.

My astounding new family has provided so much clarity into what a good and healthy family is all about. It's made me realize even more how shitty I had it growing up, and how that time of my life so naturally led to bad decisions.

These wonderful young ladies will never understand what I went through, because they will never go through it themselves.

I was assigned back-to-back tours at a major Navy training hub. One tour was spent in creating structured training products. My final tour was in a different educational setting, and the course I taught was worth eighteen transferable upper-level college credits. I am still in awe of where my journey has led me. It's overwhelming and moves me to tears every time I think about it.

Unfortunately, I developed medical problems during both of these assignments. Melanoma and pericarditis (inflammation of the pericardium, two thin layers of a sac-like tissue that surround the heart) took me out of commission for months at a time during the first tour. The pericarditis episode almost derailed my next job and nearly forced me to seek medical retirement. Fortunately, I was able to beat the stress test on numerous occasions and was able to stay in the Navy until I retired normally.

It was during my last tour that I thought I was going to die.

I was at the base clinic and I don't remember why. I do remember the nurse who took my vitals. My primary care physician wasn't in that day. The nurse was alarmed at my blood pressure but could not do anything about it there because there was no doctor available. She just sent me home for bed rest.

The next day I went to work like every other day. I was in a meeting when I started to lose my eyesight and hearing. My legs were getting numb and I announced I needed to go to the hospital. My buddy rushed me out to get help. The base clinic just calls 911 for emergencies, so he drove straight to the city hospital.

Along the way there was one delay, right at the intersection in front of the hospital—it was a funeral procession.

I looked at my buddy and said, "How funny would be if I died on my way to the hospital because of a funeral procession?" I thought I was being comical. He didn't answer me.

The hospital called for the stroke team when I explained what was wrong with me. My blood pressure was at very a dangerous level. I was in a hypertensive crisis with a possible transient ischemic attack. TIA is often called a mini-stroke, but it's really a major warning because it's a temporary blockage of blood flow to the brain.

What struck me at the time was that the numbers they called out as they worked on me were the same numbers I had when I was sent home from the clinic the day before.

I had been in a genuine hypertensive crisis and I had been sent home to rest. I could have died. *That nurse could have killed me.*

All that I'd done, all I'd suffered through in my life up to that point, meant nothing. None of the bad things, none of the good. Not the successful Navy career I'd forged out of raw despair, and not the warm embrace of my new family who loved me unconditionally. I have never forgiven that lady for her actions that day in the clinic.

I'd been shot at, been the intended target of car bombs (by default of being in range), and dodged mortars and rockets, but this was different. None of those other times was my life at risk due to incompetence. She should have called an ambulance for me.

I've been able to forgive everyone who ever wronged me in my life, so far, except her. It's something I still wrestle with. I feel sometimes I'm overreacting, but other times it puts me in a foul mood.

I decided I would retire from the Navy shortly after this frightening episode. I had reached the twenty-year mark, so I was eligible. I had two years remaining on my enlistment contract and, upon completing them I would be a civilian. I had so many great reasons to retire.

The only thing I was missing was a post-retirement plan for employment.

I was petrified of life outside of the military. I had been a failure all of my life before the Navy and I feared I would be a failure after. All of the experience and education I received while I was in uniform didn't seem to matter.

I wanted to continue doing what I was doing in adult learning administration. I was good at this and felt like this was my next calling. I have a Bachelor's degree, but it isn't in traditional education. I was a Certified Master Training Specialist in the Navy and a certified "enlisted professor" (not the actual title, but it was a title that was up for debate within the Navy), but I thought the civilian world wouldn't take these qualifications seriously. I feared I wouldn't find anything I would succeed in outside of the only world I'd known since my life surfaced from its early chaos.

My wife and I had just bought our dream home, which I feared was the dumbest decision in human history given my looming unemployment situation. Not having a post-military employment plan damned near caused me to commit suicide. Actually.

I would need to find a real job immediately ... *unless* ... a dead servicemember's government insurance is worth $400,000. If I was somehow gone my wife would get that money, and I wouldn't need to worry about her future. I didn't want to kill myself, but this thought swam around like a deadly piranha in my mind for months.

I sought psychological counseling and psychiatric care. I stopped caring about stigmas associated with mental illness a long time ago.

My wife believed in me. She kept telling me I had nothing to worry about. But I was having full-on panic attacks.

As my retirement date drew closer, the more petrified I became. I must have sent out a hundred applications for jobs. I looked into driving for Uber.

I interviewed to be an insurance salesman.

I applied for jobs I was well over-qualified for and jobs I thought were entirely out of my league.

Then I got a call from a job I thought was entirely out of my league.

CHAPTER FOURTEEN
A LEAGUE OF MY OWN

I was interviewed twice for the position I'm fortunate to hold today. My first interview was with human resources and my potential supervisor. My second interview included the chief operating officer, and a room full of other top executives. Incredibly, I was hired even before my Navy retirement date.

I had accrued a great deal of unused leave time by the end of my active duty Navy career. I used that leave to begin working in my new position, as an executive in a state agency where I'm responsible for the organization's professional development and training—and I'm crying right now. The reason why is the reason why I'm writing this book, trying to come to terms with how my life turned out this way.

After only a few months into the job, I felt like I somehow wasn't supposed to be an executive-level employee. I wasn't supposed to make it this far.

Based on my childhood and school years, I wasn't supposed to make it at all, let alone thrive. *I believed I was supposed to fail*, like every other time in my non-Navy life.

I didn't fail, and this is something I struggle with almost daily.

I have my dream job. I have a nice house in a nice town. I didn't fail. I'm the only one of four children in that fucked-up home environment who didn't fail.

I'm the only one of us with a college degree. I'm the only one not struggling with an addiction or anti-social issues. I feel like the sole survivor of some terrible cosmic accident. And it's only because I ran off and joined the Navy. Everyone else stayed home and let their lives disappear into drug dependence and hopelessness.

Do I thank my dad for this? I don't, but sometimes I think I ought to. He prepared me for success in the worst way a parent can, but I think he prepared me nonetheless. I forgave him instead. He was troubled and, in some ways, the product of his times like I'm the product of mine. That isn't an excuse, but maybe it's a reason.

My sister and brothers stayed to witness more infidelity between my mom and "dad." More violence. They stayed and fell into alcoholism and addiction and witnessed their father nearly die from an opioid overdose. He may be clean now. I have no idea. I don't remember the last time I talked to him.

This was the same man who was going to shoot me in the head if he ever caught me high on drugs—a man who said that while swilling beer by the case. The same man who was intentionally injuring himself on the job to get pills. The same man who almost died of an overdose.

I may have forgiven him for my own peace, but I will never forget the pain he wrought over a defenseless child. I visited once about a decade ago but I'll never go back. Too many memories, too much pain.

My younger brother still struggles with heroin. He has a wife and kid, and I truly hope he is able to get back on track. His wife is one of the most caring human beings I know. He is such a nice guy and has so much potential. It's painful for me to not give him money when he asks for it because I know it's for drugs.

My sister. I made my peace with her after her boyfriend nearly stabbed her to death. Remember my friend who painted my jacket so gloriously in high school? He murdered two women—an ex-girlfriend and her sister—in a blind rage over a dog he wanted returned. My sister was there with him when it happened and, in his frenzy, he started stabbing her, too. He was one or two stab wounds away from killing my sister before realizing he was stabbing his girlfriend. He was trying to patch her up when the police arrived. I called her and told her I loved her while she was recovering in the hospital.

I didn't want to visit her because she tried drinking both of her sons away and failed both times. Both of them are troubled because of her behavior. She became wildly erratic and violent. Her husband left her. She was breaking into houses to steal pills and booze. She lives off Social Security and a monthly disability check, but she still asks random friends of mine on Facebook for money because her drugs and booze eat up her rent money.

While I've made my peace with her, I'll never allow myself to be close to her again. In my eyes, she's a monster.

I hardly speak with my other brother. He had a terrible childhood too, of course, growing up amid great dysfunction, violence, and addiction. It's painful for me to speak with him because I know what he witnessed and he was set up for failure like we all were.

I think he's finally turning things around. He's moved out of my parent's basement and has a girlfriend. He was a shut-in for most of his young adult life. I don't think he's on drugs. I hope not. I hope he finds his way.

I left my mother for last for a reason. I have a hard time expressing my disappointment with her for not leaving my "dad" when she could have—*should* have. I have a hard time with her enabling her children to grow into drug addicts and alcoholics. I have a hard time expressing my disappointment in her for being so weak-minded with no sense of independence. She had very little to do with how I turned out other than my not wanting to be like her. I have broken her heart every time we talk, and it can't be helped anymore.

Until I started writing this book, my wife didn't know my whole backstory. We've been married going on seven years. There are things about my past that, if she had known them before we started dating, we might never have started dating.

It wasn't that I intentionally hid any of this, it's that I wanted to forget about all of this stuff. I stopped intentionally communicating with my family about ten years ago, and that certainly has helped me heal. I just didn't want to reopen that can of worms for my wife.

However, just as I started writing this book, a texting war between my mother and I broke out. The timing, while coincidental, helped fuel the project. The words between us only reinforced my sense of urgency in wanting to make sure my story is told. It only took about five days to write all of this.

The conversation started innocuously enough, with a text from her announcing my grandparent's house was being torn down. The timing was perfect. I wanted to make sure I had the timeline correct for this book, so I started asking a few questions. I didn't tell her I was writing a book. The conversation then turned to my childhood. That's when the conversation turned ugly and I begged her to leave me alone.

Our flame war ended with this exchange:

Mom: "This is the last thing I'm saying to you: I DIDN'T FUCKING KNOW ABOUT SHIT THAT HAPPENED WHEN I WAS AT SCHOOL OR WORK. I DIDN'T FUCKING LET ANYTHING HAPPEN. I DEFENDED YOU. YOU DON'T REMEMBER.

Me: "Did you ever think that maybe being in a relationship where you have to defend your child [from the other parent] is probably a really awful relationship? You stood right next to him in the kitchen when he would write 'Jew Boy' on my lunch bags. You didn't defend me then."

Mom: "He's too stupid to realize it was a hurtful thing. He's an idiot ... he's an asshole, yes. I should have left for lots of reasons. I coped by taking you guys out of the house all the time. I was afraid. Sorry I was soo [SIC] weak."

That she is still with this man and continues making excuses for why she can't leave is just fucking sad, and I won't be a part of it.

That's why I choose to mostly ignore her. She needs to let me go as well. This book is my closure. This book marks a moment in my life where I feel I'm finally able to let go of all this.

I've found my way, my path in life, completely on my own. I found success on my terms. I shouldn't still feel like a failure for doing so, but yeah, I'm still working on that part.

I am still under out-patient psychological and psychiatric care. I take antidepressants. I am in no way ashamed of any of this. I am respected by those I lead at work. I took a broken training program and have created a professional development program that I am introducing to all fourteen state agencies in the state I call home. I haven't even been on the job a year yet. I have a true passion for what I do in life.

Today, I have a true passion to live. If that means I take meds, so be it. If that means I need professionals to talk to, so be it. I will never again be ashamed of who I am, because I know well who I used to be.

If you can relate in any way to my story, I hope you keep working on your path.

We are not alone.

CHAPTER FIFTEEN
THE GOOD WITH THE BAD

Okay, so I exposed scandals for everyone in my family, including my own, talked about addiction hell, and glorified the military. I really didn't provide any real lessons learned yet. So, here goes.

In the words of Cato the Elder, "The wise learn more from fools than fools from the wise."

I don't remember when I first heard this saying, but it has stuck with me for many years. I've learned so much from the fools in my defective family that I learned what not to do in life. I learned how to make lessons-learned a working part of my conscience.

From my mom, mostly in their absence, I learned lessons on self-respect, integrity, fidelity, and honesty. I learned to never let someone make me feel like I have no other choice but to remain in a toxic relationship. I'm proud of her for leaving her first husband. I am absolutely disheartened by her unwillingness to leave her second. If there was ever a marriage that should have ended to protect the children, this was the one.

Keeping that marriage intact hurt everyone—including her. I would have had more respect for her if she had just taken off on her own instead of choosing to remain miserable, and the consequences of her misery cascading down to the rest of us.

I learned the importance and effectiveness of tough love. My sister belonged in jail. My mom kept bailing her out. She would have been better off in jail, where she would have had to face her problems and, hopefully, figure out how to address them. My mom would bail her out, and she would continue with her addictions and problems with the law. My mother never let my sister hit rock bottom. The older she gets the harder that eventual bottom will impact her.

I'm *glad* to have hit my rock bottom. And while I learned the importance of tough love from my mom, I learned the importance of leniency from police departments and the Navy, and countless friends for giving me many chances to do better. I didn't always deserve them, but I hope I've paid them back with interest.

Getting caught wrong, realizing my mistakes, and demonstrating these behaviors were never going to happen again has been part of my character my whole life. It's like a covenant I made with my soul. Not even sure how I was able establish this. Fear of my dad? Maybe.

I learned the importance of letting go, of not keeping people in my life who only bring darkness. I overcame an early existence of hopelessness and misery by design and no small amount of good fortune. In doing so, I reinvented myself several times.

Some of my lessons were of omission, not commission. From my dad, I learned the importance of education. I learned the importance of respecting others, especially those closest to you. I learned so fucking much from this dude.

I learned to not be a violent, angry drunk. I do still drink, lately barely at all, but I do still drink. Even at my worst, I was never violent or angry when I drank. Not sure what kind of quality is involved with a funny, responsible drunk, but I pretty much would fit in this category. I think a lot of people who know me would agree with this assessment.

As I've reached a point in life I am almost entirely comfortable with, I find myself drinking less. Early on, I always had used drugs and alcohol to escape my life. Today I don't want to miss anything. I embrace every moment of every day with excitement, especially when it comes to my amazing wife and beautiful daughters, our four dogs and five cats.

I learned almost accidentally that pornography is poison and can be more damaging to relationships than some chemical addictions. Being exposed to pornography as young as I was still very much fucks with my head. Sex is difficult because I have trouble being in the moment. I find myself comparing the act with what my brain has previously seen as erotic, and the pornographic dissonance gets in the way.

You may notice I didn't mention the other person involved in sex. I noticed it, too. I'm sometimes too caught up to pay attention to that most important part. I'm working on this problem. I wish I had not seen so much hardcore porn without first having sex. I wonder how different my brain would be. I wonder how much happier I would be.

I have learned to be opened-minded, and tolerant of others. Aside from my first encounter with Iraqi people (who we were at war with), I don't negatively judge anyone because of what they look like or how they live their lives. I learned the value of "to each their own."

I also learned the value of discipline. While my own choice was to join the Navy, I don't want you to get the impression that the military is the only path for someone at rock bottom. There are many roads to success. The key is to prepare yourself for the trip.

From my uncle, I learned to have a healthy sense of humor. I learned the importance of taking time to have fun in life. I think he played a large part in my behaviors with alcohol as well. If you're going to be a drunk, be a funny drunk. I also learned to appreciate the beauty of the outdoors and natural sciences. I learned how to fish, navigate mountain trails, and to enjoy a mountain swimming hole.

From my grandparents, I learned genuine love. They were an amazing couple who deeply loved each other. They did their own things and they did things together, but they were always a team. I will never forget the sense of warmth and comfort I felt with them. I felt accepted. I felt protected. They had the relationship I actually prayed for. Today, I have that relationship. I often still can't believe how my life has turned out.

About my brothers and sister, I wish they'd learn from my mistakes. I hope none of them choose to stay in the quagmires they're trapped in.

Oddly enough, I learned the importance of commitment from my sister, and why sexual fantasies should sometimes just remain as fantasy.

She and her husband had a foursome (not the golf kind) with another couple they were close with and it ruined their marriage. Her husband has a great career, they had a nice home in a rural town. My sister had a good job at a bank. The breakup destroyed my sister and she was never able to recover.

They tried to make their marriage work, but it was doomed. My sister got pregnant shortly after the foursome. She had already been drinking heavily and the pregnancy didn't slow her down. She continued to drink vodka like water—to include sleeping with a fifth of it every night.

She was too cowardly or simply too afraid to terminate the pregnancy, so she callously tried drinking her baby away. It didn't work, and today that child has issues related to her drinking.

After her inevitable divorce, she became pregnant again in a relationship with a crack addict. She tried drinking that baby away, too. I haven't seen that kid since he was an infant, but it's clear through photos that her drug use and booze have impacted his childhood development as well.

I have certainly learned from my own mistakes. I still do. I do my best to make sure they don't return. The biggest lesson learned is to seek help when it's needed. Over time—and the Navy helped—I also learned to keep myself entertained and try to stay focused on the positive; always try to provide a solution along with a problem. I learned the importance of communicating ideas to assist others.

This is pretty much what gave me the balls to finally write this book. I learned to ask for help and do research to find the answers I need. I never think I have all of them.

I never will.

NATIONAL SUICIDE PREVENTION LIFELINE™

1-800-273-TALK

www.suicidepreventionlifeline.org

facebook.com/samhsa   @samhsagov

SAMHSA

Substance Abuse and Mental Health
Services Administration

877-726-4727

The National Domestic Violence

HOTLINE

1.800.799.SAFE (7233) • 1.800.787.3224 (TTY)

ACKNOWLEDGMENTS

First and foremost, I want to take a moment to thank my wife. She is my favorite person on Earth. I want to thank my daughters, who love me unconditionally and have accepted me in their lives. I could not love these people with any greater depth.

I also want to thank the following people.

Retired police detective RW and the department he retired from, for showing me tough love, understanding, and for helping me find direction—but most importantly for believing in me.

Thanks to the teachers who took their personal time to help me get my education back on track. I wouldn't be here without them.

My "townie" friends who did their best to shield me from misery. We may not have done things the right way, but we did what we thought was right at the time.

The U.S. Navy, for so many opportunities to learn and grow, and for trusting me and empowering me to fill leadership roles beyond any I could have imagined. I will always remain in awe of the Navy Chief Petty Officers who shaped me. I will always treasure my memories of the officers and Sailors who challenged me to find creative solutions to impossible problems.

The state agency I work for took a chance on an outsider and welcomed me like family. I could not be happier with what I do in life.

The psychologists, counselors, and psychiatrists who showed genuine interest in helping me reconcile my past and present.

And last, but by no means least, my brother Navy Chief, friend, editor and book designer (who prefers to remain anonymous) who helped me dig deeper until I felt I had nothing more to add to this story.

I may or may not ever reveal my true identity. I ask those who know my story to please allow me to make this decision on my own terms.

I love you all.

BMFB
January 2019

Bio

The pseudonymous *Baby Mountain Flower Bear* was born and grew up on the East Coast of the United States with a sister, two brothers, and occasional pets.

He spent twenty-two years in the United States Navy and retired with honors.

LEGAL

The author has tried to accurately recreate events, locales, and conversations from his memories of them. In order to maintain anonymity, in some instances he has eliminated the names of individuals and places. He may have changed some identifying characteristics and details such as the order of events, physical properties, occupations, places of residence, and other factors not affecting the accurate telling of his true story.

This story has not been reviewed for classification by the U.S. Navy.

CPSIA information can be obtained
at www.ICGtesting.com
Printed in the USA
BVHW071821290419
546834BV00009B/1191/P